Inside Out Transformation®
presents

The Energetics of Money Liberation™

6 Steps for Finding and Releasing Your Blocks to Experiencing Financial Liberation NOW!

Linda Humphreys, PhD

THE ENERGETICS OF MONEY LIBERATION™
6 Steps for Finding and Releasing Your Blocks to Experiencing Financial Liberation NOW!

DrLindaHumphreys.com
Published by Inside Out Transformation, LLC

Unless otherwise noted, all Bible quotations are from the King James version (KJV), accessed through www.biblehub.com.

Parts of Chapters 11, 12, and 14 are taken from *Getting God® ~ "The GOD Project"—6 Steps to Divining Your Way to A More Intimate and Loving Relationship with God* by Linda Humphreys, PhD © 2019.

ISBN-13: 978-0-9724161-6-0

Interior Designer: Pam Terry, Opus 1 Design
Editor: Candace Johnson; Proofreader: Michelle C. Booth;
Front Cover Original Graphic Artist: Paitoonpati;
Cover Designers: Linda Humphreys and Erik Allen;
Back Cover Photographer: Melody Barooni

Printed in the United States of America

This book is dedicated to
Seekers,
Believers in redemption,
more than second chances—and choosing again, Dreamers,
Strivers,
Transformers,
Visionaries,
Way-Showers,
and
Those who persist in the quest of capital "T" Truth both Within and
Throughout—
in everything and everyone.

Yesterday I was clever, so I wanted to change the world.
Today I am wise, so I am changing myself.
—Rumi

What lies behind us and what lies before us
are tiny compared to what lies within us.
—Ralph Waldo Emerson

Are you able to receive merely "pennies" from Heaven …
or are you ready—
as a child of the Most High—
to receive your divine birthright inheritance,
which can include
money liberation and financial prosperity?
—Dr. Linda Humphreys

Contents

Preface

I am an intuitive coach, metaphysical / energy clearing facilitator, consultant, and author. I do not diagnose and/or treat medical, financial, and/or psychological issues, nor are the contents in this book and the accompanying *PLAY*book meant to diagnose and/or treat these issues. The work I do and the information presented within this book and *The Energetics of Money Liberation*™ ~ *The* PLAY*book—Support for Your Money Liberation Project* are not a substitute for medical attention and care, psychological counseling, financial consulting, financial counseling, legal advice, and/or psychiatric care.

I assist with the identification and releasing of hidden or underlying energetic blocks and imbalances. In particular, I work with blocks and imbalances that may contribute to and influence one's emotional and physical energetic and may contribute to one's mindset as well as spiritual, financial, and relationship issues and challenges.

My goal and intention are to assist you in identifying, clearing, and releasing stuck energy in service to your emotional, physical, mental, energetic, spiritual, and financial well-being. Additionally, I want to help you gain clearer access and connection to your unique Divine Healer within.

No guarantees, but the more you remove energetic blocks and imbalances, the better chance your body, mind / mindset, and emotions have to be at optimal and supportive functioning—allowing your True Self to shine through.

How to Get Optimal Results

Being open-minded and open and receptive to healing—for your highest and greatest benefit and for the highest and greatest benefit of everyone on the planet—is key to experiencing optimal results.

I am very clear that God / Spirit / Highest Power / Big Love does the healing work.

What to Expect after a Clearing and Releasing Session

After a session has been completed, be gentle with yourself because you will be going through a readjustment period. Your energetic system will try to re-alchemize to a less internally burdened and encumbered state. This readjustment period can last a few days. Some symptoms may include emotional sensitivity, crying, difficulty sleeping, becoming sleepy, need for extra sleep, and vivid dreams. Or you may experience nothing at all.

Although results vary from person to person, these are some of the ways people have benefited from doing this work as it relates to finances:

- Greater inner peace
- Stronger sense of connection to God / Spirit / Highest Power
- Greater feeling of safety and security
- Greater sense of being in the flow
- Increased awareness of what abundance and financial prosperity are—and what these means to them
- Greater compassion for themselves and their journey
- Greater experience of being more open and receptive to the flow of energy—in the form of money
- Better able to be receptive to the inflow of energy in the form of money
- A deeper understanding of the importance of *money liberation* and financial prosperity—in service not only to their own lives and the lives of their families but in service to supporting other individuals and humanitarian organizations as well

BOTTOM LINE: Be gentle on yourself. Just as you would be extra gentle with yourself after a physical surgery, consider these sessions as a type of energetic surgery. Allow your system to recalibrate to a new state of homeostasis and equilibrium. Rest and drink plenty of water.

Also, establish a mindset of gratitude. Cultivate gratitude for everything and everyone. Everything you have ever experienced has brought to you to this moment—a very fine place to be and a great moment to begin your *money liberation.*

And so it is.

Introduction

The topics of abundance and prosperity have been a long-standing source of interest, curiosity, confusion, frustration, and, ultimately, inspiration for me. Throughout the years, I have put considerable thought and energy into the pursuit of my own abundance and prosperity. I have attended workshops, read books, developed and recited mantras and affirmations, and created vision boards and ideal scenes, just to name a few.

After much introspection, I can see that the root of my interest began with my family of origin—particularly with my parents' teachings, attitudes, belief systems, dynamics, and manifestations concerning *abundance* and finances.

My parents were children during the Great Depression. Both were impacted by the economics of the time. What my parents learned and taught me: you must work very hard, save your money "for a rainy day," and rarely spend it because "you will never have enough."

Growing up, I noticed disparities and contrasts between financial prosperity and lack of money, viewing those around me in terms of the haves versus the have-nots. When I was young, I became determined to be one of the haves and not remain a have-not.

In spite of their self-perception and attitude of being have-nots, my parents began to accumulate a vast array of antiques and collectibles. Our home quickly became more of a storage place of boxes of things than an actual living area. Even the hallways and stairs were filled with stacks of books and boxes. We had an overabundance of things, yet the mantra of "never having enough" was pervasive the entire time.

Later in life, I gravitated to the metaphysical (simple meaning: beyond the physical) texts. I was drawn to the positive and proactive nature of the teachings. I read everything I could about the *law of attraction*, *abundance*, *co-creation*, and *manifestation*—all in an attempt to rid myself of being a have-not. Try as I might, things did not go as quickly or as big as I wanted; confusion, anger, frustration, fear, and disappointment set in. After some time, I decided to analyze my experiences, evaluate what worked, seek inner guidance, and create a success mindset and the tools to achieve a more financially prosperous experience in my life.

Money Liberation and Financial Prosperity

I believe it is God's / Spirit's / Highest Power's intention for us to have a life flow without blocks—in all aspects of life—including experiencing *money liberation* and financial prosperity.

For the purposes of establishing a common frame of reference, I will use one of Dictionary.com's definitions of *prosperous* as "having or characterized by financial success or good fortune; flourishing; successful."

I also believe that God wants us to experience forms of *abundance*, using this definition of the noun from Dictionary.com: "An extremely plentiful or oversufficient quantity or supply; overflowing fullness"—including the experience of an abundance of financial resources—and even more specifically: money.

I contend there is a separate and distinct difference between abundance and financial prosperity. In my opinion, the generic and vague term *abundance* is overused, undefined, and proliferated in popular self-help literature. For those eager to improve their level of financial standing, I believe the vagueness of the term *abundance* contributes to the detriment, confusion, frustration, anger, fear, pressure, and lack of manifesting optimal results—particularly and specifically regarding achieving actual financial prosperity and experiencing greater financial freedom.

In this book, I intend to provide specific ways in which you can gain a clearer understanding, mastery, and empowerment in what I term Abundance vs. Prosperity Consciousness.[1] I believe

---

[1] "Abundance vs. Prosperity Consciousness©" is the title of my thesis for one of my master's degrees.

the clarity and distinction offered here, along with practical tools and easily achievable action steps in this book and in the companion *PLAY*book, are imperative to achieving greater awareness and inner peace for individuals, and, ultimately, for a more peaceful and harmonious society.

In the next chapter, I provide a survey of popular metaphysical literature to illustrate how the term *abundance* is used. In later chapters, I provide suggestions for approaching abundance and financial prosperity—separately and together—with clear and specific additional components to add as fuel.

Additionally, I provide information and specific tips, tools, and techniques that you can use to discover, release, and clear your energetic blocks and imbalances—both conscious and unconscious—toward achieving financial prosperity and ultimately experiencing financial liberation.

This is my gift to you. I offer it with my intention and prayer: to assist you with manifesting what is for your highest and best benefit, for yourself, others, and the entire planet—and for those that want to experience true financial freedom—specifically, financial liberation.

Namaste.

PART I

MY EXPLORATION:
AN OVERABUNDANCE
OF
ABUNDANCE

Chapter 1

Examining Abundance

In 2016, Chapman University conducted a survey of America's top fears.

> [A] random sample of 1,511 adults from across the United States were asked their level of fear about 79 different fears across a huge variety of topics ranging from crime, the government, disasters, personal anxieties, technology and many others." One of the eleven major domains included in the study was "Personal Future," which included concerns about "dying, illness, running out of money, unemployment." With an "Average Fear Score" of 4, "Personal Future" ranked 1.95. The percent of Americans who reported "being afraid or very afraid of running out of money" was 37.4 percent. This fear even beat public speaking ("Personal Anxiety" domain: 28.4 percent) and dying ("Personal Future": 21.9 percent).

The high percentage of fear people expressed about money—specifically the fear of running out of it—seems to indicate a belief that money is limited or finite in supply—at least for them. If that perception is not the case, I wondered, why the fear?

I asked people I knew some questions about their views of money, specifically to see what, if any, fear-based beliefs were attached to their perceptions. What I noticed: almost everyone did have some fear associated with money ("losing it," "running out of it").

Then I asked, what are you doing about that belief? Some of the answers were: "Hoping for the best," "Keeping my fingers crossed," "Praying that doesn't happen," and "Practicing manifesting abundance."

That last phrase, *practicing manifesting abundance*, puzzled me. It also piqued my interest, so I decided to explore what, exactly, that phrase meant—and how to do exactly that: *manifest abundance.*

My Research Exploration into Manifesting Abundance

What I found was a significant amount of manifestation literature.

After surveying the internet and reading countless bloggers' "Best Self-Help Books" lists, two out of the top ten books were consistently abundance-related: *The Law of Attraction* by Esther and Jerry Hicks and *The Secret* by Rhonda Byrne. Another best-selling book, though not mentioned in any of the lists, also mentions manifesting abundance and living abundantly: *The Holy Bible.*

Needless to say, people tend to have great fear surrounding the topic of finances. In my internet research, I also found countless abundance websites and even abundance-related movements, organizations, networks, and communities. The central message of these best-selling books, blogs, networks, and communities (and other popular books and messages from modern-day gurus in the metaphysical and spiritual arenas) have more than just the theme of abundance in common: they lack clarity, and they inaccurately use the word abundance itself.

An Overabundance of Abundance

In my examination of literature, I decided to begin with an often-quoted passage from the best-selling book of all time, *The Holy Bible.* John 10:10 (New King James Version), states: "The thief does not come, except to steal, and to kill, and to destroy. I have come that they might have life, and have *it* more abundantly."

What does "have life and have it abundantly" mean? Of the fifty -four different Bible translations available at Biblegateway.com, thirty-four used the same word: *abundantly.*

Matthew 13:12 (New International Version) states: "Whoever has will be given more, and they will have an abundance. Whoever does not have, even what they have will be taken from them." Rhonda Byrne, author of *The Secret* and other books related to the metaphysical, including *The Magic* (considered #3 in a series of The Secret books), added words to Matthew: "Whoever has gratitude will be given more, and he or she will have an abundance. Whoever does not have gratitude, even what he or she has will be taken from him or her." (Byrne, 3)

Byrnes's addition of the word *gratitude* does not, in my opinion, add any clarity to exactly what abundance means in this context. Though she uses the word *more*, what, exactly, does she mean more of?

Byrne also writes, "Your gratitude is magnetic, and the more gratitude you have, the more abundance you magnetize. It is Universal law!" (Byrne, p. 5)

In both of the examples above, "more abundance" and "have an abundance" are extremely vague. When one has gratitude, what, exactly, will one be attracting or magnetizing? If one has gratitude, what, precisely, will they have an abundance of?

Laws

I also believe that using the term *law* adds to confusion, frustration, fear, and anger when applied to personal finances, as it makes the concept even more ominous and foreboding.

While there are laws based on honed observation and repeated and verifiable scientific experimentation, such as the law of gravity, my mind and emotions latch onto another kind of *law*. As a result of how I wired the word *law* within my own mind, I connected that word to penal laws that must be obeyed. My perception and reaction resulted in creating internal stress.

Universally, if one does not follow a *law* or breaks a *law*, there is an inherent implication of punishment. Even if that is not the author's intention when using the word in this context, the word triggered and activated my subliminal or unconscious interpretations, misperceptions, beliefs, and stresses—and it may affect other readers the same way.

There are negative consequences to pay if one breaks the law in our society. Additionally, in the religion I was born and raised in, there were also negative consequences and eternal negative punishment for not following God's laws. I learned that any violation of God's laws has much more severe and dire consequences—as punishment can last for a literal eternity.

A plethora of books unite the word *law* with the concept of attracting success, abundance, loving relationships, and so on. Some examples of such *law* books include *The Law of Attraction* (Esther and Jerry Hicks 2006), *The Law of Divine Compensation* (Marianne Williamson 2012), and *The Law of Success* (Napoleon Hill 2011).

If one adds God to the mix—and if there is a perception or misperception that one has violated one of God's *laws*—additional or heightened anxiety may be caused—and that is what happened within me. In this scenario—coupled with the perception / misperception of *law* being connected to penal law—if a universal law is violated, one could possibly be punished (by God, by the Universe). A potential punishment could be not receiving abundance. This type of conscious and/or subconscious thinking can lead to questions such as:

- Is God a punitive God who keeps financial prosperity away from people?
- Is God withholding money as a weapon or a form of punishment?
- What does one do "wrong" to incur God's withholding of money?

Being Vague Is in Vogue

Within the same *abundance* texts I read and have cited previously, the use of the word *gratitude* is also a bit vague and not well defined. I have asked people to define what gratitude means to them. Their universal response was "being grateful." No one ever responded in a more emotionally descriptive way. Their responses seemed rote—and lacking of any semblance of emotion.

The vague and obscure term *abundance* also appears in the writings and vernacular of other modern-day self-help gurus. Goodreads.com lists numerous quotes about abundance, including "When you are grateful, fear disappears and abundance appears" by Anthony Robbins, author of books such as *Awaken the Giant Within*, and "Seek abundance and you will find abundance" by Suze Orman, financial advisor, media personality, and author of books such as *The Courage to Be Rich*. In *Become a Better You: 7 Keys to Improving Your Life Every Day*, American preacher and televangelist Joel Osteen (2009) writes, "God wants you to succeed; He created you to live abundantly." Additionally, in *Your Best Life Now: 7 Steps to Living at Your Full Potential*, he writes, "If you develop an image of victory, success, health, abundance, joy, peace, and happiness, nothing on earth will be able to hold those things from you."

What, exactly, I wonder, should I have an image *of* when trying to imagine abundance?

Sandy Forster, owner of the website Wildly Wealthy and a self-described "best-selling author … world traveler extraordinaire and mentor to over 55,000 women all over the planet" writes, "It's not enough to know or even write about abundance, you must be abundance, you must live abundance."

I was not able to find any guidance, definition, or instruction for how to "be abundance" and "live abundance" within the text of her website.

In fact, in all the texts cited, I was not able to find any definition or explanation of the term *abundance*. While financial prosperity may be their intended connotation, that is never clearly nor directly stated.

What I was able to find were broad, sweeping, general statements, without clear and specific guidance and focus, leading to an abundance of confusion, frustration, and dismay.

Chapter 2

Abundance Means What, *Exactly*?

How can I "be abundance"? How can I "live abundance"? How can I be and live something so ambiguous, nebulous, and amorphous?

I decided to conduct an unofficial survey of some friends. When I asked what *abundance* means to them, their responses were, "a lot of," "a plethora of," "lots and lots," "tons of," and so on. All the terms they provided seemed to me to be more of an adjective that modifies a noun.

How the Word Abundance Is Misused

I looked for appearances of *abundance* in the Bible. In John 10:10 I found the statement "have life, and have it more abundantly."

According to Dictionary.com, *abundantly* is an adverb. An adverb enhances or gives a descriptor of a verb. A verb is an action word. "Have" is the verb in the sentence in question. To have "it" more abundantly, is, in essence, to have a plethora of … what, *exactly*?

As I mentioned in Chapter 1, Dictionary.com's first definition of the noun form, *abundance*, is "an extremely plentiful or over sufficient quantity or supply." When a word can act as either the noun or a descriptor (adjective) in need of a noun with which to enhance or describe that noun (for example, "an abundance of __________" —my mind wonders, "an extremely plentiful or over sufficient quantity or supply" of what?!

Affirming Abundance

In some of the classes and webinars I took over the years, I was constantly told to affirm *abundance*. This is another phrase that I regularly came across during my exploration journey about *abundance* that confused me.

Here is an example of what got triggered in my mind and my subsequent thoughts whenever I was told to *affirm abundance*:

> So … when I affirm abundance, to me, it is like affirming … red (as an example). If I affirm more red, … is that what I want, exactly? Is that exactly what I want to experience? What, exactly, is the experience of red? Would I know, exactly, when I am experiencing red? How do I quantify red? How will I know when I achieve red? Will I know that when red shows up, it is exactly a manifestation of my affirmations?

Are you confused? That's exactly my point: I was lost.

My point is that modern-day gurus, life coaches, preachers, metaphysicians, spiritual practitioners, self-help presenters, and authors (just to name a few) are using or have been using the word *abundance* as *the one and only* noun—such as in the term *affirm abundance*. However, another use of the word *abundance* is as an adjectival phrase that includes the object of the noun. Here are some examples: abundance of money, an abundance of time, an abundance of love, and so on.

Every time I heard the term *affirm abundance*, especially without being given additional guidance and/or information in the metaphysical materials, my mind would become distracted with thinking: an abundance of what?!

I do not recall coming across or experiencing any guidance or instruction about being specific when told to *affirm abundance*.

Potential Reasons Why Abundance Is Misused

The fact that an abundance-related term appears in thirty-four of fifty-four Bible translations (biblehub.com) may be an example of what happens in the game Telephone, where an error gets passed down from person to person. In this case, an error in translation may have been passed down from one Bible translation that affected subsequent translations. Going unchecked and unquestioned has resulted in its continuing use today.

Much like the game Telephone, the word *abundance* seems to be used again and again in today's metaphysical popular literature and vernacular—passed down and picked up by one guru and incorporated by new gurus without explanation or clarification. As a student of the metaphysical community, this lack of clarity contributed to some of my own frustration and fear regarding my personal finances.

Negative Consequences of the Abundance Movement

When the metaphysical community communicates about manifesting, the word most often used is abundance. It seems to be a catchall for … I am not *exactly* sure what. Based on my review of self-help literature and resources, I am not sure anyone really knows—or has not been able to explicitly and clearly communicate exactly what they mean. I believe the use of such an ambiguous term as abundance (exclusively) and the lack of direct and specific focus can contribute to the creation and/or perpetuation of frustration and disappointment. I experienced that frustration and disappointment and other negative emotions, and I know that other people trying to implement the teaching of *abundance* and *affirming abundance* experience the same kind of negativity.

The energy of frustration and disappointment, if left to linger, can contribute to fear and anger toward one's self, others, life in general—and even directed toward God. It can also contribute to other vibration energies even lower than frustration and disappointment.

When considering one's personal finances, the same frustration and disappointment, when combined with the fear factors noted in the Chapman University study, can lead to general negativity, shaming, blaming, and stress. It can also lead to negative reactions that can negatively influence neutral and/or supportive decision-making about one's finances and financial behaviors such spending, saving, and investing money.

These negative elements can have dire internal and external consequences. Negative thoughts and feelings, if allowed to persist, do harm both within (an individual) and throughout (society). If one tends to react in an inward / internal fashion toward financial negativity, frustration, and so on, a bleak internal environment can be the result. Based on my personal experience, it can lead to

- worry and doubt regarding connection with God / Spirit;
- anxiety;
- doing things "right";
- being "wrong"; and/or
- doing things "wrong"—just to name a few things.

Reacting in an inward fashion can also lead to what I call *New Age guilt*, a unique way of blaming one's consciousness for not being able to manifest the desired result. This may also display as stress-induced dis-ease (examples include high blood pressure, ulcers, and migraines) and self-blame. Based on personal experience, I know that this type of stress, if left to linger, can cause both an inward and outward stress reaction, a fight / flight / freeze response. I experienced all three, caused by the constant inner stress I created within myself.

Seeking an outward person, place, or thing on which to hang blame for lack of financial resources—in spite of one's efforts and/or due to lack of efforts—results in an absence of taking personal responsibility or ownership for oneself. Ultimately, negative internal influences (thinking) coupled with outward blame-seeking thinking and subsequent blaming behaviors toward outside forces (people, places, and things)—leads to reacting as a victim.

My Experience of the Misuse of Abundance

In addition to experiencing frustration and fear about my personal finances, I experienced what I call "New Age guilt." I became masterful at using my perceived lack after trying very hard, and I turned inward, using my negativity as an opportunity—a weapon—with which to beat myself up. Ultimately, this contributed to self-hatred. I began to think, *If I am personally responsible for everything that manifests or does not manifest in my life, what is in my consciousness to manifest lack? Why have I not manifested improved finances? What am I doing wrong?*

My underlying thoughts and fears were:

- What is wrong with me?
- Am I a "bad" person?
- Is God punishing me?

Additionally, when I experienced my version of a fight / fright / freeze response, it presented as fear, anger, worry, and doubt.

- I feared the worst and felt anger against myself for getting into a specific situation.
- I worried that I could not pull myself out of the situation and/or God would not pull me.
- I doubted my "position" with God.

I asked:

- "Will God bless me with money?"
- "Will God abandon me and ignore my prayers?"
- "Is God angry with me?" and so on.

From there, negative internal tirades against myself, my life—even against God—began to spin from within. I thought:

- Why was I not "blessed"?
- Am I not meditating enough?
- Am I not praying "correctly"?
- What am I doing "wrong"?
- I am grateful! Am I not grateful enough?

- Did I break a universal law?
- Am I being punished for breaking a law?

If I had been surveyed for the Chapman University study, my fear scale would have been so high it would have altered their results to indicate a higher fear score because of personal finances!

At that time, I perceived God as outside of myself—and I was angry and frustrated with God for not answering my prayers. Praying, chanting, reciting mantras, and creating wish lists did not seem to work for me. They did not deliver what I was asking for—nor did God. As a result, I began punishing myself (internally) and feeling punished by God (externally). As this continued, I experienced increased fear and anger within myself and toward external things, people, events—and still experienced a lack of what I was seeking: money.

Fear, anger, confusion, frustration, and doubt were my constant inner companions—and they colored my inner world. They colored my perception of myself and my perception of my position as it related with God. I kept questioning where I stood. Was God listening to me? Ignoring me? Playing with me? Messing with me?

My negative emotions also tainted my experience of and attitudes toward my outside world. Here is a sampling of what I thought and felt:

- I am not safe.
- Achieving financial security is a struggle.
- I have to expend effort and work hard to achieve anything and everything.
- I have to do it all alone.
- Figuring this out—and achieving abundance—is a struggle, and I am struggling.

Chapter 3

Why It Is Vital to Declutter Abundance

In the early 1900s in Germany, political forces blamed "The Jews" as the chief source and cause of the country's economic hard times. Dire and heinous events followed.

Given the modeling of the bullying, unfriendly, and blaming nature of our current political and social models and events, an individual's financial stress and fear can contribute to a more hostile, negative, blaming, and outwardly aggressive stance toward and exchange with others.

Seeing parallels (energetic, vibrationally, and in a myriad of other ways) to Germany of the early to mid-1900s and the political climate of the United States at this time, I feel that we, as individuals, need to gain clarity, empowerment, and success in taking personal responsibility for what we can control: our focus, thoughts, and actions. We need to gain mastery of these instead of perpetuating blaming and victimhood.

Several years ago, I was watching a television interview of members of what was then a newly emerging social and political movement that called themselves "a modern-day Tea Party." A married couple in that interview said something that struck me. They described themselves as "fearful, angry people." When asked by the interviewer what they were angry about, they responded, "The economy! Our jobs! Our money! Our homes! *Everything* is being taken away from us!"

Over time, the "fearful, angry people" movement—for a lack of a better word—has intensified and increased; one striking example is the January 6, 2021 insurgence in Washington, DC. This phenomenon, however, is not exclusive to the United States. Fear and anger, which appear to be the new pandemic, have escalated and need to be eradicated as soon as possible. It is part of what I call a *spiritual pandemic* that affects every part of an individual's life—and spreads like wildfire into all aspects of society around the world.

Other symptoms of this pandemic include victimhood and blaming—with degrading and throwing shade. Reluctance to take personal responsibility—on any level—has made some people resemble guided missiles of scorn, contempt, rage, jealousy, and envy (to name a few). They seek a target of others—those outside of themselves who are different or foreign to them socially, politically, physically, sexually, and so on—to become the target of their obsessive, all-consuming blind rage.

I believe that if more people did take personal responsibility and gained mastery with clear and specific tools to achieve greater financial prosperity, we would have less of an abundance of fearful, angry people voting for politicians who incited negativity and reactivity in the form of blaming others and entrenching victimhood and anger, which, as we have recently experienced, has incited violent protests in the process. By practicing specificity in my own life around my personal finances, my inner fear and anger have dissipated greatly. I am experiencing greater inner peace.

One of the key elements of my *practice of specificity* includes using specifying words and visualizing specifically what I desire. If, for example, I want more money, I actually use the word *money* (and not only the word *abundance*). Additionally, I specify what *more* means to me. I then use specifying words and images that relate to those specific words—in my visualizations, affirmations, and *declaring and claiming* statements.

I find it increasing alarming that more and more programs such as public radio and government agencies charged to protect us are in the crosshairs of the aforementioned politicians and risk being majorly cut to having total government support taken away. These and other environmental and humanitarian-centric programs and agencies must rely, now more than ever, on sponsors and individual donors. The more individuals experience a positive income flow the more likely they are to donate to causes and programs they believe in that have touched their hearts and they want to support.

Society as a whole needs clarity, direction, and proven, positive results in many areas in life—including improving individuals' personal finances. Based on my experience and the experience of others I have supported in their quest for financial freedom, people are more inclined to be calm, less stressed, and become more financially philanthropic when they feel empowered—and empowerment includes being financially secure. This contributes to helping individuals, society, the country, and the planet as a whole.

Chapter 4

Books, Drums, and Rockets for Aspiring "Haves"

A study conducted by the United Nations University's World Institute for Development Economics (UNU-WIDER) reported the following:

> The richest 2% of adults in the world own more than half of global household wealth ... The most comprehensive study of personal wealth ever undertaken also reports that the richest 1% of adults alone owned 40% of global assets in the year 2000, and that the richest 10% of adults accounted for 85% of the world total. In contrast, the bottom half of the world adult population owned barely 1% of global wealth.

If you do an online search of the word *abundance*, you will find a proliferation of books, materials, websites, workshops, and so on. Given the amount of material devoted to the subject, it is surprising that those percentages have not fluctuated over time to include a higher percentage of wealthy people—or is it?

A 2009 *Forbes* article titled, "What People Are Still Willing to Pay For" included the following:

> Americans spent $11 billion in 2008 on self-improvement books, CDs, seminars, coaching and stress-management programs—13.6% more than they did back in 2005, according to Marketdata Enterprises, an independent Tampa-based research firm that tracks everything from adoption agencies to funeral homes.

A 2014 article titled "The Self-Help Industry Helps Itself to Billions of Dollars," author Lindsay Meyers, MBA, MPH, writes,

> Self-improvement represents a $10 billion per year industry in the U.S. alone. In addition to high revenues, self-help also has a high recidivism rate, with the most likely purchaser of a self-help book being the same person who purchased one already in the last 18 months. This begs the question of how much good these self-help books and seminars are doing for consumers. If they are so effective at solving our problems, why do they usually result in a continuing stream of self-help purchases?

By 2019, according to the latest information from NPD Bookscan, which tracks the US publishing market, the self-help category was also becoming more crowded.

> The self-help books category has experienced continued and solid growth in recent years. In fact, it has nearly doubled in size since 2013. Unit sales of self-help books have grown at a compound annual growth rate (CAGR) of 11 percent since 2013, reaching 18.6 million in 2019.

When I read the above, one thing that struck me is this: every eighteen months, people purchase more / other self-help books. Several reasons could account for this:

- They are avid readers of this genre.
- They want to improve themselves.
- They have not yet attained what they are looking for.
- They are seeking a source outside of themselves for information and support—and have not yet acquired what they are seeking.

Again, there may be other reasons, but these are the four that occurred to me.

Additionally, the increase of sales and publishing numbers in subsequent years within that genre no doubt indicates people are purchasing even more books and within even shorter time spans.

With the proliferation of general abundance materials, workshops, websites, and such, (again, as evidenced by an online search), it seems that those who are attaining actual financial prosperity are those who tout having the solution and market such materials, vague though they may be. I believe they are actually selling hope, possibility, and potential.

What Does Not Work

Financial abundance won't come through blaming someone or something anything outside of oneself, including

- society;
- birth order;
- social status at birth;
- race;
- ethnicity;
- gender;
- "others" such as migrants and immigrants;
- bad luck; or
- one's lot in life.

Perceiving yourself as a have-not is such an easy and convenient way of perpetuating a victim mentality and avoiding the need to take proactive measures toward personal improvement—on all levels.

I believe that, as evidenced with the increase of book sales within the self-help genre, aspiring "haves" want—and are motivated—to change their present and perceived have-not experience of their lives. They are motivated to purchase books that focus on helping improve themselves and the conditions and circumstances they are currently experiencing. It seems as though they are taking personal responsibility (helping one's *self* through *self*-help books) and realizing that changes can be made by going within.

While going within may be challenging and hard to face, I believe one's "fix" focus needs to be placed *internally*, by first and foremost taking personal responsibility. Additionally, by utilizing specific tools and techniques—for example, being specific and focused about goals and desires—one can more successfully achieve the intended and specific things desired.

Without clearly and precisely directing direct and energetic attention, the adage "garbage in equals garbage out" could be modified to:

Ambiguity, Uncertainty, Vagueness Within
Equals
Ambiguity, Uncertainty, Vagueness Throughout.

But with clarity and direct focus, I say:

"Clarity and laser-focused intended results within
Equals
Clarity and laser-focused intended results throughout."

What Does Work—and the First Step in Achieving Success

I've listened many times to an audio cassette tape recording of a live lecture that took place in Arizona on March 19, 2005, which is a "channeled" session of "Abraham," a self-described "collective" of "Spirit Guides" by Esther Hicks. In it, Abraham talks about applying specific focus in this way: "You beat your drum, and the Universe will respond to the drum that you are beating …" I believe it would behoove those wanting financial prosperity to see if that is indeed the exact drum they are actually beating.

In *The Vortex: Where the Law of Attraction Assembles All Cooperative Relationships* by Esther and Jerry Hicks (2009),

Abraham discusses beating the drum of what one does not want. By examining what is not wanted, we can gain clarity and realize what we do want. However, Abraham advises us not to stay and linger on what is not wanted. Lingering in the not-wanted energy and mindset can lead to separation between the self and what one intends to manifest, and to separation between one's self and, ultimately, others.

An example of putting energy into the present condition and not the intended and desired outcome is wanting a change "over here"; focusing on what is lacking "over here"; joining support "clubs" about being "over here"—all the while desiring to be "over there."

Another illustration and metaphor that Abraham uses is "rockets of desire." According to Abraham, when we experience contrast (such as have-not vs. have), a rocket of desire is launched. Though the contrast contains useful information, Abraham cautions not to linger in the energy and focus of the undesired results, which will, in turn, set off rockets of desire and a beating of the drum for what is not wanted.

A literal rocket requires both precision and fuel with which to reach the desired target and produce the desired outcome. Unguided rockets do not reach their intended targets—which can cause undesired and negative consequences. According to Abraham, the same is true regarding the "energetic rockets of desire" that we launch. Abraham advises to be clear and specific regarding the desired and intended specifics to produce desired, intended, and specific results.

By being clear and specific and focusing on discovering unconscious / subconscious blocks and imbalances around financial prosperity, I am offering a system of energetic releasing techniques that is different from what you'll find in other self-help books. Next I will explain some of those techniques.

Chapter 5

And So It Is

Words have a specific and distinct energy and vibration. The work done by Dr. Masaru Emoto, researcher and author of *The Hidden Messages in Water*, and accompanying photographs he took of water crystals, shows a correlation between consciousness, focused attention and energy, vibrations, and its effect on matter.

In a more historical document, the Bible, the power of the Word is everything, as demonstrated in often-quoted verses:

> *"In the beginning was the Word, and the Word was with God, and the Word was God." (NIV, John 1:1)*
>
> *"The Word became flesh and made his dwelling among us..." (NIV John 1:14)*

Several years ago, I took a course about the metaphysical interpretation of the Bible. Just to be clear with my words, and to assist with your clarity of understanding what I am about to share, I want to provide you with my definition of the word *metaphysical* as I understand and use it.

Metaphysical simply means beyond the physical, and more specifically, it means beyond the literal. It is used quite often when speaking about energy and vibration, as something in the realm of metaphysics is beyond what most people's physical eyes can see.

In the metaphysical interpretation of the Bible class, this passage was explored. This is what I gleaned from my studies:

1. God had a thought.
2. God's thought became Word.
3. God's Word manifested into the physical realm.
4. The physical creation manifested resided in the physical realm.

Stated another way:

1. We—an extension of God called *souls*—can think a thought.
2. Our thoughts inspire / inform our words.
3. Our words have the power to create what we experience.
4. We are living the consequences and effects of what we have created.

Not to belabor the point, but to state it even more succinctly:

1. Watch what you think—and how much fuel (time, energy, and attention) you are giving it.
2. Take care with what you say and how you say it.
3. What you state becomes your experience—your reality.
4. Your reality is a result of your thoughts, words, and feelings; feelings about your own thoughts and your own words—and those of others.

I would also like to add:

You are capable of changing
what you perceive as your reality.

Words and Vibrations

Another source of energy for words, fuel, and power is *emotions* (*energy in motion*). Specifically, emotions that are wired or paired with certain words or phrases within someone, the energy with which the words are delivered, and the energy that accompanies the words. Another way of thinking about it is that your words are a vehicle and emotions are the gasoline.

Here is an example of how the energy of words works: upon hearing certain words and/or a certain delivery of certain words, an internal (within) emotional trigger can be set off within the receiver. This can cause an emotional response or reaction when received.

Also worth noting: Even if the person delivering those certain words is in a neutral energy state and delivers those words in a neutral manner, the receiver still can react due to being triggered within. I can personally attest to this phenomenon—both as a receiver and deliverer of certain words and phrases.

There is an idiom that states, "Your word is law." I always found that to be a very powerful statement. Contemplating the meaning of this statement led to deep introspection about what I actually set up as laws for myself. This exploration led to the discovery of what I was actually saying to myself (internally) and to others (externally).

My Financial Laws

"I can't afford that!" and "That's too expensive!" were two of the major statements I told myself. Those statements were my laws—my affirming of lack within my mind and, ultimately, creating my experience. The drums I was beating and the rockets I was launching were those of lack and less than:

- I did not have enough money to afford things.
- I was not rich—coupled with the feeling of feeling poor—literally and metaphorically.

Literally, I was poor financially because of my law of not being able to afford things. Metaphorically, I felt a twinge of victimhood in the pit of my stomach: poor me. And so it was.

The major lesson I learned as a result of my introspection was this: if my own word is law, I have to be specific in exactly what I want to experience. I have to be clear in my thinking, attitude, emotions, and actions. I have to be clear about what I desire, *what* I am communicating, and *how* I am communicating it

- within myself (internally);
- to the Universe (through my actions, attitudes, perceptions); and
- when I am communicating with others.

Also, while being introspective about my financial status, I became conscious of certain words, blocks, and barriers I had placed between me and the flow of financial prosperity. Additionally, I began to wonder about the blocks and barriers within my subconscious or unconscious awareness:

- What subconsciously / unconsciously was I telling myself about money?
- What had I paired or wired together as triggers?
- What programs and/or blocks had been subliminally instilled and, up to now, remain hidden?

My quest continued …

PART II

MY EPIPHANIES

AND

INSIGHTS

Chapter 6

My Abundance Epiphany

It became abundantly clear to me that saying I wanted abundance—or 'an abundance of all that is good' in my prayers, affirmations and mantras—helped me to manifest a bunch of really cool stuff. However, I never—specifically—manifested what I really wanted at the time: more money.

Lesson learned: If my intention is to manifest something specific—be specific with thoughts, words, and energy focus.

—Dr. Linda Humphreys

After driving home from work late one night, I found myself embroiled in one of my negative, internal (and what I call) spins from within. At that time, my home was in a very affluent part of Southern California. Although I lived in what I termed "the everyday people's section," it was still in one of the richest areas in the county—perhaps even one of the richest per capita in the country, as well.

As I followed a turn of the road, I saw something that would alter my perception of abundance forever. I saw what was, arguably, the one and only homeless person in the entire town (at that time), pushing a grocery cart. Not only was the cart filled to the brim—it was stacked nine feet high!

There it was—before my very eyes. I had found "it"; I had found abundance. That woman was abundantly ... abundant. She was living abundantly; she was able to be abundance; she was exactly what everyone in my information research wrote about. That formerly vague and illusive concept now had a visual I could relate to.

In that moment, I realized that I have been getting exactly what I have been affirming, praying for, stating to God, the Universe, and to anyone / everyone who would listen: *ABUNDANCE!*

I had an abundance of examples of my experiences of abundance:

- My dining room table was filled with paper, books, and newspapers—*abundance.*
- The trunk of my car was filled with dry goods, books, and magazines—*abundance.*
- The back seat of my car was filled with a crate of water bottles, magazines, and newspapers—*abundance.*
- The floor of my closet was cluttered with shoes, boots, clothes to give away, clothes to take to the dry cleaners—*ABUNDANCE.*

It then dawned on me that I had re-created the same energetic and dynamic of my family of origin. I, too, had an overabundance of things ... stuff—yet the mantra of never having enough was pervasive the entire time. Because I had been focusing on *abundance*, I got exactly that—*ABUNDANCE.*

Additionally, I realized that after using the generic word *abundance* or the phrase *an abundance of all that is good* in my affirmation statements, verbalizations, and so on, I did not manifest more money. I also realized that money was what I intended to manifest, though I never used the word *money* in any form.

I wondered:

- Why don't I receive more money?
- What part of me is blocking myself from perceiving that money does not fit into the categories of *abundance* or *an abundance of all that is good*?
- Is my mind wired to think (subconsciously / unconsciously) that money is

  - not part of abundance or an abundance of all that is good?
  - *not* "good"?
  - "bad"?
- Why am I resistant to using the word *money* in my thoughts, intentions, prayers, meditations, affirmations, and so on?
- How can I change my thinking, affirmations, vibrations, and manifestations?

More questions and epiphanies followed ...

Chapter 7

Money

Everything in life is vibration.
—Albert Einstein

Other than having a physical vibration like a piece of metal (as in coins) or a piece of paper (dollar bills), money has neither a specific vibration nor a hierarchy of vibration on a scale of energetic vibration. (Hawkins, 2012)

Some people may protest: "How can that be? Money is one of *the* most powerful things on this planet."

Where money gets its power and what gives money its *power* is within each and every individual. Many things add fuel and internally amplify our inner dialogue about money, including our

- thoughts;
- feelings / emotions;
- memories of our past;
- upbringing;
- training / education;
- religion;
- life experiences;
- messages absorbed through media of all forms;
- and so on.

All the elements above empower one's perspective and attitude—and ultimately, one's actions *plus* reactions—toward money. Money gets fueled from within. What is mentally and emotionally—consciously and/or subconsciously (or unconsciously)—generated from within individuals informs and influences one's attitude and perspective—and perhaps, even negative judgment—toward those who have money and those who don't. It can also add to negative judgment against how people choose to spend money—or how they don't. And judgment in not just reserved for others. Sometimes the harshest judgment is toward and against one's self.

As a collective or society, we all have consciously and subconsciously / unconsciously made some kind of an agreement (by way of actions, thoughts, and so on) that there are money haves and money have-nots. While it may, indeed, be a statistical fact that 10 percent of the population owns the wealth in the United States, there are those who view that as a foreshadowing of their destiny: they are—and will forever remain—a have-not.

Some people seem doomed to re-create their past and accept their status quo. Others seem to transcend and alter outlooks, perceptions, perspectives, and limitations prescribed by others.

I opened this chapter with a quote from Albert Einstein: "Everything in life is vibration." Vibration is an energy—so another way of stating this is, "Everything in life is energy." With this in mind, emotion or e-motion (energy in motion) is, what I call a *self-generated internal state energetic*. As such, our thoughts can trigger a self-generated internal state (emotion) that can lead to a reaction.

Another way of stating this is:

Unconscious and/or Conscious Thoughts

+

Reactions

Lead to

Emotions

(Self-Generated Energy)

Your thoughts, emotions, and reactions about everything—including money—or your perceived lack of money *plus* your reactions to it all—are an energetic choice.

You have power over money; money does not have power over you. How are you choosing to empower yourself—as it relates to money—today? What self-generated internal state (e-motion) will you choose to experience today? Financial self-entrapment and bondage … or money mastery and liberation?

Make your choice today.

Chapter 8

God

I believe the challenge of our perception—and misperception—
of our relationship with God is both universal and pandemic.
This disconnection with the Divine contributes to
dissonance and discord on the planet.
As such, this requires immediate attention and healing.

—Dr. Linda Humphreys
Getting God® ~ "The GOD Project"

While you may think that a chapter about God / Spirit / Your Highest Power in the content of a book about money is incongruent—or even sacrilegious—I propose that it is the polar opposite. I believe it is only until you grasp and experience the True Nature of God—and clean up your relationship with Your Highest Power—you will, most likely, prolong your longing, searching, frustration—and perhaps even anger.

Unless and until you think of God as a benevolent, loving, and supportive God who

- has your back;
- is on your side;
- wants you to succeed—on all levels and in all aspects of your life; and
- adores you;

and unless and until you think of yourself as

- a daughter or son of the Divine;
- inherently deserving;
- innately worthy;

- not needing to prove you are worthy;
- not having to work hard to earn God's love;
- already blessed; and
- a grateful receiver,

you are only damning and dooming yourself to a life sentence of perpetual constriction and restriction—in all things—including money.

I believe that owning your connection with
God / Spirit / Highest Power—
the Divine Within—
and owning your Inner Divinity
(which serves to activate your
Spiritual DNA—Divine Nature Always)
are key to experiencing inner healing,
transformation, and miracles.

—Dr. Linda Humphreys

Philosopher and Jesuit priest Pierre Teilhard de Chardin wrote, "We are not human beings having a spiritual experience. We are spiritual beings having a human experience." I believe that unless and until you are able to truly embrace and embody this concept, the desires of your heart—including but not limited to *money liberation*—will remain elusive and as distant as you may currently perceive God to be.

One of my favorite quotes was, I believe, channeled by God / Spirit / Highest Power through Marianne Williamson in her seminal book, *A Return to Love*:

> Our deepest fear is not that we are inadequate. Our deepest fear is that we are powerful beyond measure. It is our light, not our darkness that most frightens us. We ask ourselves, Who am I to be brilliant, gorgeous, talented, fabulous? Actually, who are you *not* to be? You are a child of God. Your playing small does not serve the world. There is nothing enlightened about shrinking so that other people won't feel insecure around you. We are all meant to shine, as children do. We were born to make manifest the glory of God that is within us. It's not just in some of us; it's in everyone. And as we let our own light shine, we unconsciously give other people permission to do the same. As we are liberated from our own fear, our presence automatically liberates others.

To this day, this quote inspires, delights, and informs some of my thoughts, actions, and, most definitely, meditations. These words have truly become words to live by.

Chapter 9

God and Money—and You

Take delight in the LORD, and God will give you the desires of your heart.

—Psalm 37:4

This is the book, program, time, day—and even the moment—to once and for all release any and all misconceptions and misperceptions as it relates to God, money—and you. To end the cycle and separation you are currently experiencing, the following thoughts, misperceptions, and emotions / energy must be released:

- powerlessness;
- hopelessness;
- unworthiness;
- undeserving;
- not being humble enough;
- lacking;
- limitation; and
- regret.

All of the above can be summed up with this one concept: victimhood.

"Poor me" can figuratively—and literally—become your life's experience: *poor* you. Additionally, thoughts and words such as "I am just a poor sinner" can result in exactly that—affirming and entrenching you are a sinner who is poor.

There is truth within some common aphorisms:

- As above—so below.

- Garbage in—garbage out.
- What you focus on—expands.

I also say:

- "So within—so throughout."
- "Whatever is inside—spills to the outside."
- "Energy grows where attention goes."

Another common expression is "food for thought." With this in mind:

- What thoughts are you feeding?
- What are you feeding your thoughts?

Within the context or framework of God and money—and you—are you feeding your mind junk food? Here are some examples of junk food:

- God is punishing me.
- God doesn't like me.
- God doesn't love me.
- God doesn't listen to my prayers.
- I must do something to earn God's blessing of more money.
- It is sinful to have too much money.
- It is more spiritual to be poor.
- Being rich is sinful—and money can lead to more sinning.
- Money and me are just not meant to be.
- Not being rich is my lot in life.
- I have to work harder to earn more money.
- Having money is not being humble.
- The only way to make good money is to do something illegal and/or immoral.

Or ... are you feeding your thoughts health food?

- God is on my side.
- God wants me to be happy, healthy, and financially prosperous.
- I trust myself to make wise investments.
- I am a generous and giving person—and I can contribute to organizations and causes that are near and dear to my heart.

The food you are feeding your thoughts may be both conscious and subconscious / unconscious. Now is the time to explore both to make sure that what you are using is productive in a way that enhances your life—and that you are not just piling on a boatload of s#!t for fertilizer.

So don't be afraid, little flock.
For it gives your Father great happiness to give you the Kingdom.

—Luke 12:32

Chapter 10

Your Money Relationship

We are never not in a relationship.
We are in relationship with everyone and everything—
at all times— including a relationship with money.

—Dr. Linda Humphreys

Using the context of a relationship, when you view money, how is your relationship going?

Start by asking yourself questions about your relationship with money. Here are some queries to consider:

Are you and money

- solid?
- on good terms?
- amicable?
- close?
- a source of joy?
- having fun?

Or are things

- a bit rocky?
- turbulent?
- distant?
- antagonistic?
- a source of stress and strife?

All relationships—including your relationship with money—require awareness, time, attention, care, and so on to develop, blossom, and thrive.

Your Money Tree

When I was growing up, often in response to me expressing a desire to purchase something, my parents would often respond by saying, "Money doesn't grow on trees."

However, imagine that money actually *did* grow on trees, and you had your own personal money tree. Keeping this image in mind, here are some queries to consider:

- How is your relationship with you and your money tree?
    - Are you nurturing and tending to it, or are you ignoring it and hoping for the best? Are you cultivating it with positive nutrients—in the form of positive thoughts, words, feelings / vibrations, or are you shoveling too much manure—in the form of negative thoughts, words, feelings / vibrations—and too much "BS" from your negative money story?
- Does sharing the positive story of your money tree entice others to partner with you and help you nurture and grow it?
    - Is your rendition enticing and desirable for other people to partner with you and help you nurture and grow it, or is your story rendition repelling other people from partnering with you and helping you nurture and grow it?

Relationship Approaches

I have discovered that how people approach money is, more often than not, indicative and reflective of how they approach life—and love.

Here is a sampling of some money-relationship personalities and approaches I have encountered when working with clients and some of the traits associated with them.

Hope-for-the-Best: magical thinking, wishful thinking, affirming for the best, wistful imagining without taking any proactive action steps.

Waiting-to-Be-Rescued: fantasies of winning the lottery, waiting for a rich relative to leave something in their will, hoping for a rich relative, focusing on marrying rich, winning big at a casino.

The Money Victim: focus and identity based on what happens(ed) "to" them, blaming others / things for being stuck financially, no real and committed proactive steps taken to transform a poor financial situation.

Other approaches include Afraid and Frozen, Eyes Shut, I'll Show You, I Told Me So, Bad Boy / Bad Girl, and Money Martyr.

To learn more about Money Relationship Approaches—
and how you approach your money relationship—visit
DrLindaHumphreys.com/Money-Relationships

How You Are with Money

Have you ever heard the saying, "As you are with ____________, so you are with life"? I've often observed this aphorism in action in different contexts.

I also believe that "As you are with money, so you are with life—*and* love."

So ... how are you doing in the money, life, and love departments in your life?

PART III

UNSEEN FORCES

AND

INFLUENCES

Chapter 11

Energy Centers

If you want to find the secrets of the universe, think in terms of energy, frequency, and vibration.

—Nikola Tesla

Another aspect within the realm of the unconscious / subconscious is the *Energy Body*. These subtle energies are what constitute one's aura, prana, and qi (or chi).

Below is a brief introduction to energy centers that can affect you as energy relates to anything—and everything—including your relationship with money.

Energy Body

Barbara Ann Brennan, author of *Hands of Light*, writes about the seven components of the Energy Body:

- **Etheric:** Extends one-quarter to two inches from the physical body. This is what is captured in Kirlian photography[2].
- **Emotional:** Extends one to three inches from the physical body.
- **Mental Energy:** Stores our mental processes, judgments, perceptions, and thoughts. This energy extends three to eight inches from the physical body.
- **Astral Body:** Assists in the detection of more subtle energy perceptions. It extends six inches to one foot from one's physical body.

[2] Kirlian photography is a process in which an image is obtained by application of a high-frequency electrical field to an object (such as a leaf of metal coin) so that it radiates a characteristic pattern of luminescence that is recorded on photographic film.

- **Etheric Template Body:** The template from which the body is formed—like a blueprint. The extension is one and a half to two feet from one's body.
- **Celestial Body:** Described as the spiritual emotional plane. When we experience "The Oneness," spiritual bliss, and both inner- and inter-connections (between you and others), we are connected to the celestial body via this bridge to the Divine.
- **Ketheric Template Body:** Described as the mental aspect of the spiritual plane. All of the other bodies are contained within this body, with an extension of up to three and a half feet. We experience this template when we experience our "Divine Knowing."

Chakras

Chakras are energy centers. Some people refer to chakras as the spiritual spine. Here are the basics from Chakras.info:

> Originating from Sanskrit, [chakras] literally means "wheel" by association with its function as a vortex of spinning energy interacting with various physiological and neurological systems in the body. Chakras are energy centers within the human body that help to regulate all its processes, from organ function to the immune system and emotions. We can commonly count 7 chakras positioned throughout your body, from the base of your spine to the crown of your head. Each chakra has its own vibrational frequency, that is depicted through a specific chakra color, and governs specific functions that help make you, well, human.

The seven chakras are:[3]

[3] This is a compilation of what I have learned and studied throughout the years from various sources and resources. The Connections column is a partial, cursory listing of properties, gifts, and attributes connected with each chakra.

Chakra Name	Color	Position	Connections
Root	red	base of spine	grounding, survival, safety
Sacral	orange	below navel	creativity, sexuality, relationships, emotions
Solar Plexus	yellow	stomach	personal power, will, confidence
Heart	green	center of chest	love, empathy, compassion
Throat	blue	base of throat	creative self-expression, speaking one's truth
Brow (Third Eye)	indigo	forehead, above & between eyes	insight, wisdom, inner vision, intuition
Crown	violet / white	top of head	higher consciousness, connection with the Divine

Though I have listed seven chakras, I have heard that there is actually a total of twelve known chakras. I believe there may even be more.

Meridians

According to the teachings of traditional Chinese medicine (TCM), meridian systems (channels or pathways of energy, also known as qi or chi) are the pathways along which the body's vital energy flows. They can also be thought of as a collection of acupuncture points.

There are twelve principal meridians and eight extra meridians. The governing meridian is among the extra meridians, and as such it is viewed as among the most important channels. Its importance is derived from the independent nature of its acupuncture points—which are not part of the twelve principal meridians.

If you drew a line of the governing meridian, it would run from the center of your upper lip, up the center of the nose and forehead, over the center of the head, down the center spine, and end at the tailbone.

Your Fingertips

The tips of your fingers emit energy, as is evidenced by Kirlian photography. They are a powerful tool and used in a variety of healing modalities. Your fingertips are elements that can facilitate remarkable transformation when placed on energy points and combined with the power of your declarations, humility (stepping aside), higher vibration states of energy (gratitude, openness), and God / Spirit / Highest Power. They are the tools that are utilized within my own *Money Liberation Project*—to support the release of negative subconscious programming.

***

In the next chapters, I explain how working with energy centers can assist in unlocking the secrets of your inner subconscious universe.

Chapter 12

Exploring Unseen Forces and Influences with Divining

How fathomless the mystery of the Unseen is!

—Guy de Maupassant

Wondering what was within my subconscious (which was running 95 percent of my own habits and behaviors) within my energy field—and wondering how that applied to my perceived relationship with money—I decided to literally test myself.

Proof via a Lie Detector

I set out to explore the best and most efficient way to do this. I often thought, *If I could find some kind of a detector test, would that be the way to do it?* At that time, the only testing I knew of was using an actual lie detector. Half-jokingly and half-seriously, I looked into the concept and the mechanics of the lie detector device.

The Lie Detector (As I Understand It)

In very simple terms, this is what I learned.

- Our bodies and energy fields respond to unseen forces and influences.
- The nervous system is the channel of electrical energy and controls skeletal muscles.
- When something resonates with us (such as a truthful statement, a thought, specific feeling), we have a physiological response to it via the nervous system.
- When there is dissonance with something, we have a physiological response to it as well.

- In addition to changes in breathing patterns and heart rate, a physiological response can be in the form of micro muscle movements.
- A lie detector test is formally called the Galvanic Skin Response Test.
- This testing device can detect physiological responses, including micro muscle movements and the flow of energy.
- These micro muscle movements and the flow of energy are tracked via graphing.
- A baseline of resonance (truth) and the presence of dissonance (falsehood) can be discerned and are the first things discerned.
- Upon questioning, if there is resonance (truth) present, no marked movements of micro muscles are detected. The lines on the graph will be stable. This indicates that there is no disruption or obstruction of the flow of energy. It is equivalent to getting an affirmative response.
- Upon questioning, if there is dissonance (falsehood) present, marked micro muscle movements are detectable. The lines on the graph dip downward and waiver. This indicates that there is a disruption or obstruction in the flow of electrical energy, resulting in blocked energy. It is equivalent to getting a "not affirmative" response.

Not having a Galvanic Skin Response device at my disposal, I searched for other ways to discern resonance and dissonance within myself—especially as it related to what was running my subconscious show regarding my perceived relationship with God. My search led me to find exactly what I was looking for—a modality that is:

- accurate;
- practical;

- portable;
- something I could quickly and easily master;
- something I could do myself or could find support for; and
- not prohibitive financially.

Divining / Applied Kinesiology / Muscle Testing

The best and most accurate way I have found to test one's energy field and unconscious / subconscious programming is commonly called *muscle testing* or *applied kinesiology (AK)*. Regardless of what it is called, I believe it is a form of divining.[4]

While researching the mechanics behind the practice, I learned that the energy that causes weakening of muscles when performing AK / muscle testing / divining is also the same energy that propels the swinging of the pendulum (another modality of resonance and dissonance detection and a form of divining). All of the above modalities operate using the same theory and energy that cause results detected by the Galvanic Skin Response device.

Mechanics of Divining / AK / Muscle Testing (As I Understand It)

In very simple terms, this is what I learned (note that there is overlap with the lie detection process):

- Our bodies and energy fields respond to unseen forces and influences.
- The nervous system is the channel of electrical energy and controls skeletal muscles.
- When there is resonance with something (for example, a truthful statement, a thought), we can have a physiological response to it.

[4] I find it interesting that certain forms of applied kinesiology (AK) are referred to as "divining" or "divination" (examples include divining rod and dowsing rod). I truly believe the word "divination" does have a root (literally and metaphorically) with the Divine. I view AK as a gift from the Divine with which to access the Divine Knowing Within.

- When there is dissonance with something, we can have a physiological response to it as well.
- In addition to changes in breathing patterns and heart rate, a physiological response can be in the form of micro muscle movements.
- Divining can detect changes in the micro muscle movements and the flow of energy.
- With divining, a baseline of resonance (truth) and the presence of dissonance (falsehood) can be discerned and are the first things discerned.
- Upon questioning, if there is resonance (truth) present, no marked movements of micro muscles are detected; electrical energy flows freely and the muscles will test strong. This indicates that there is no disruption or obstruction of the flow of energy and no blocked energy. It is equivalent to getting an affirmative response.
- Upon questioning, if there is dissonance (falsehood) present, marked micro muscle movements are detected. This indicates a disruption or obstruction in the flow of electrical energy, resulting in blocked energy, causing the muscles to test weak. It is equivalent to getting a "not affirmative" response.

You can test your energetic alignment with physical, tangible things (such as a food or a supplement) and intangible things (like thoughts, ideas, or emotions). This type of testing helps you decipher whether something is *energetically* congruent / beneficial / in resonance with / or present (as it relates to thoughts, ideas, emotions) for you and your energy system—resulting in a *strong* or *yes* response.

Additionally, you can use this form of testing to help you decipher whether something is *energetically* incongruent / not beneficial / in dissonance with / or not present (as it relates to thoughts, ideas, emotions) for you and your energy system—resulting in a *weak* or *not strong* response.

Divining as a Money Liberation Tool

I consider the tool of divining to be my personal and portable lie detector. Like a lie detector, it discerns truth / resonance and falsehood / dissonance. Additionally, divining is a tool that can be used to discover and discern energetic blocks and imbalances that are present within your subconscious / unconscious and your energy field.

In the context of the *Money Liberation Project*, divining is used to discover what negative and/or challenging beliefs / programs, blocks, and imbalances are present that contribute to a perceived distance and dissonance between you and money. Additionally, you can use divining techniques to discover which positive beliefs / programs are missing—and contributing to your perception of not experiencing your desired positive relationship with money.

How to Divine

There are over a dozen ways to conduct divining / AK / muscle testing without having to use a lie detector / Galvanic Skin Response apparatus. You can have another person facilitate the divining, or you can divine by yourself. In Chapter 19, you will learn one example each of two methods—one that requires two people and another method that you can do by yourself. Additional methods are explained in *The Energetics of Money Liberation ~ The* PLAY*book for Your Money Liberation Project.*

Chapter 13

Use Your Words

Say what you mean—and mean what you say—is a supportive life and communication practice. It is also a tool you can use to assist you in achieving greater financial freedom—and money liberation.

—Dr. Linda Humphreys

Oh my goodness!

I could go on and on about this topic. However, for the purposes of brevity, specificity, practicality—and particularly, as it relates to *money liberation*, I will share with you what I like to call my *Readers Digest Condensed* version of some essential energetics.

First, if you specifically want to be in receiving mode as it relates to finances, *use your words*. Ask for what you want.

Next, stop

- acting and thinking that the word *m-o-n-e-y* is a dirty, five-letter word;
- affirming and only using the vague term *abundance* in your prayers, intention, *declaring and claiming*, meditations, and so on—when you *specifically* want to experience *money liberation* and financial prosperity—because you think you are being more spiritual by using the word *abundance* instead of *money*; and
- being defensive, making excuses, and saying things like
  - "I meant that." (What, exactly, does "that" mean? It may mean different things to different people.)
  - "I want abundance—including financial abundance—and that is what I mean."

- "Financial prosperity is part of abundance."
- "I don't need to say it [money]. Financial prosperity is implied."

Instead, start being clear and precise, by

- using direct and specific words;
- saying what you mean; and
- meaning what you say.

The Power of Precision

Imagine this: you offer to do my grocery shopping. I gratefully accept. You then ask me for a list of what I want.

Now imagine the list I hand you has one word on it: *Abundance.*

Wouldn't you want to know

- what, exactly, you should get;
- how much of each item should you get; and
- how much money should you be spending?

What, exactly, would you put in the cart?

To me, the word *abundance* means "a lot." If the situation was reversed, and if I was doing the supplying (shopping), I would want to know, *exactly,* what are the parameters.

Using the same scenario as above, I would want to know, *exactly*

- what should I be providing (purchasing);
- how much of each item should I be providing (purchasing); and
- what is the dollar amount to spend?

If you, directedly and specifically, want to experience a significant increase in the money department of your life—and experience true money liberation—start by doing this: **STOP AFFIRMING ABUNDANCE!**

—Dr. Linda Humphreys

What, Exactly, Are Your Parameters?

Your definition of *abundance* and your parameters of abundance may—or may not—be the same as my definition and parameters. There is no one universal or specific understanding of the term abundance—other than meaning "a lot." This means that you should, in all forms of thinking and communicating, express exactly what you are seeking and want to experience.

BOTTOM LINE: I am going to say to you what parents tend to tell children at times when their child is not clear, is reacting nonverbally, is frustrated, and so on:

"Use your words."

Specificity in your communication—and particularly the practice of using your words—is an especially useful tool when you experience any kind of negative or reactive emotion, thought, or image when you are not receiving and/or experiencing what you are wanting, praying for, setting intentions for, meditating about, saying affirmations about, and so on.

Defining Terms on Your Own Terms

Being wealthy and/or rich may mean different things to different people. When I ask my clients to define what these terms mean to them, their initial response tends to be ... the sound of crickets.

Some people are taken aback and do not know how to respond when asked, exactly, what certain terms means to them.

I then ask them to imagine in their mind,

- Is there a dollar amount attached?
- What, if any, images come forward about this term?
- If you closed your eyes, took a few moments to go within, and answered from a deeper level, what would your response be?
- Do your definitions include:
    - inspired ideas?

- connections?
- serendipities?
- synchronicities?
- opportunities?
- intuition?

All of the latter six listings—and more—can lead to *money liberation* and financial prosperities.

How about you? How do you define being

- wealthy?
- rich?
- abundant?
- financially prosperous?

How would you define *money liberation*? How would you define other terms you use?

Again—use your words.

Ask for What You Want

Throughout my religious upbringing, I would often hear this:

"So I say to you: Ask and it will be given to you; seek and you will find; knock and the door will be opened to you."

(Luke 11:9 NIV)

With this in mind, I am an advocate of the following acronym of ASK:

*Ask: be specific, direct, clear, decisive

*Seek: opportunities, collaborations, and creative solutions

*Knock: clearly, persistently, boldly

Another way to define the same acronym—and how to practice ASK-ing—is as follows:

*Affirm: After stating your desired outcome, say "I affirm this or some things even greater than I can image, for the greater good for myself and all involved in this situation" (or something like that).

*Speak: Use words of gratitude, upliftment, kindness, support—to and for yourself (internally)—to others (externally), and Spirit (throughout).

*Know: Feel and acknowledge with assuredness that the Universe / God / Your Higher Power has your back and is on your side.

Now … use your words—and ASK!

Chapter 14

Energy Tools and Qualities of Transformation

Always bear in mind that your resolution to succeed is more important than any one thing.

—Abraham Lincoln

Setting intentions is something frequently mentioned and practiced of self-help books, workshops, conferences, metaphysical materials, and the like. When I first began my inward journey, I would physically bristle when I heard that phrase.

Wanting to explore why I was reacting in such a way, I did some reflection. I soon realized that the concept of *intentions* had confused me for a very long time. I struggled to understand why people would set intentions, what setting intentions actually means, and how to set intentions in an effective manner. I was also challenged with finding the appropriate vibration / energy that would enhance my intentions.

Setting Intentions

As I shared in one of my other books, *Getting God® ~ "The GOD Project"—6 Steps for Divining Your Way to a More Intimate and Loving Relationship with God*, the religious *Baltimore Catechism* textbooks had a strong influence on me and left strong impressions with me. One of the sayings I remember seeing in a religious book was, "The road to hell is paved with good intentions." Along with that saying was an illustration of a stairway. On each of the outward-facing sides of the stairs was the word *Intention*. The area at the top of the staircase was labeled *Heaven*, with the obligatory white clouds, angels, and God portrayed as an old man with a white beard who was sitting down and watching what was happening below. The bottom of the stairway led to what was labeled *Hell*, with the obligatory flames, red and horned demons with pitchforks, and, of course, Satan.

Fast-forward to the time of great popularity and focus on manifesting things, which came to the forefront with the popularity of the book and the movie *The Secret*. Books and workshops about manifestation, laws of attracting things, affirmations and mantra creations, and recitations were prominent in metaphysical circles. At that time, I still had the energetic vibrations of the imagery from the *Baltimore Catechism* running rampant inside of me. When I was asked to state a simple intention to manifest something, I would frequently say, "There is no way in *hell* I would *ever* set an intention. I could end up in hell—because even good intentions can lead me straight to hell!"

I thought of all of the times I had intentions and said I would do something and, for whatever reason, whatever I was intending to happen did not come about. I realized that I did not follow through, I forgot about my intentions, and so on. Upon deeper reflection, I realized I was using my intentions as yet another weapon against myself—especially about *not* manifesting something. *New Age guilt* can be just as inwardly insidious and brutal as Catholic guilt.

I would set the intention to do something—fast, meditate, journal—as a way to get something to physically manifest in my life (increases in my bank accounts, relationships), and I was always using it as a bargaining chip, a quid pro quo, a leverage tool with God / the Universe. Energetically, it was as if I were stating to God / the Universe, "I'll do X if you do / give me Y."

I now realize that intentions do carry energy: the energy in which they are created, the energy of the words used, the energy in which they are held by the person creating the intention, and the energy directed toward the intended goal. This energy warrants conscious exploration and, in some cases, adjustment.

Energetic adjustment can be made to put something more in

alignment not only with the desired outcome, but in keeping the highest and best benefit for both the intention setter and for those affected by and involved with the intention.

Intentions are meant to be stated in an affirmative way. That means, instead of stating what you *don't* want and using the word *not*, state what you *do* want. An example: instead of stating "My intention is *not* to be so disconnected from money"—state *experiencing connection with money*: "My intention is to be connected with money."

Energetic Qualities of Intentions / Energetically Directed Goals

- Direct / positive / affirmative focus
- Direct / positive / affirmative wording
- Commitment to being open and vulnerable
- Commitment to transformation
- Willingness / flexibility / adaptability
- Grounding in the here and now
- Projection of positive energy and the image of a positive outcome into your future

***Examples of Intentions*[5]**

- It is my intention to receive a regular influx of money.
- My intention is to experience gratefully receiving vast amounts of money on a regular basis.

Even More Powerful: *Declaring and Claiming*

I am highly sensitive to words, vibration, language, and energy. Having said that, I have discovered, vibrationally and energetically, the act of what I call "declaring and claiming."

---

[5] In *The Energetics of Money Liberation ~ The* PLAY*book—Support for Your Money Liberation Project*, I offer detailed guidance for creating the most effective intentions—and all of the other energetic tools suggested—that relate to achieving financial prosperity. I also provide more examples.

If you were to imagine, on a scale of one to ten (with ten being the highest and one being the lowest), the power—or what I like to call the "oomph"—behind intentions when compared to *declaring and claiming*, you would experience:

Intentions = 5
Declaring and Claiming = 10

Energetic Qualities of *Declaring and Claiming*

- Positive / supportive / powerful / strong / affirming wording
- Certainty
- Conviction
- Clarity
- A sense of excitement / delight / fun!
- Grounding in the here and now
- Projection of positive energy *now*
- Imagining successful outcomes propelling you into your future

Examples of Declaring and Claiming Statements

- I am experiencing financial prosperity *now*!
- Vast sums of money are gravitating to me!
- I *love* sharing my wealth with organizations and programs that are important to me!

Affirmations

Affirmations are positive statements. The purpose of using affirmations is to anchor the positive energy of your intentions in the here and now, and to project it into the future. Additionally, by using some specific wording, they can support greater energetic alignment with your intentions and your *declaring and claiming.*

There is a huge energetic difference between wishful thinking and an affirmation. Wishful thinking begins with phrases such as "I want to," "I hope to," "It would be nice if," and so on. These statements of a longing for something to happen—have the energy of wishful thinking which is wistful, weak, and contains a sense of doubt. Also, using these phrases, leaves a lot of space for the energy of something *not* to happen because the implied energy is "It would be nice if it happens, *but* ..."

Energy of Affirmations

Every time the word or even the unconscious / subconscious / conscious energy of the word *but* is used in these types of statements, you create conflicting or competing energies. You do not want to leave any invitation for conflicting or competing energies when creating affirmations because they negate those affirmations.

To create energetically strong affirmations, some specific wording can be beneficial. I found the following helpful when creating my affirmations:

- Begin each sentence with "I Am." This is done to call forward the God / Spirit / Highest Power / I AM presence within you and align it with the God / Spirit / Highest Power / I Am presence throughout. Using "I Am" instead of "I will" or "I am going to" supports being in the here and now, and does not postpone things into a nebulous and/or unspecified future.

- State the action word or verb in the present / present-progressive tense. Another way of stating this is to use verbs that end with *-ing* (enjoy*ing*, play*ing*, danc*ing*). This supports anchoring the energy in the here and now, and paves the way, energetically, for your future. (See *Examples of Affirmations* on the next page.)

Another key element of affirmations is to keep them within the realm of possibility for you. Some workshops and training programs

I have attended suggest creating affirmations using this guideline: make them (at least) 50 percent possible or believable. For example, "I am graduating from medical school with honors" won't work for me because I have no medical aptitude and am squeamish at the sight of blood. That affirmation is *not* within the realm of possibility nor is it something that is believable to me.

Having said that, I do believe in miracles, and I always avail myself to being open and receptive for miracles at all times. I feel it is important for you to do the same.

Energetic Qualities of Affirmations

- Positive / supportive / uplifting / affirming wording
- Commitment to transformation
- Openness / willingness / flexibility / adaptability
- Grounding in the here and now
- Projection of positive energy and the image of successful outcomes into your future

Examples of Affirmations

- "I Am open and receptive to transforming my relationship with money in an easy and gentle manner."
- "I Am enjoying sharing my financial prosperity with others."

NOTE: As I perceive it, the difference between intentions, *declaring and claiming*, and affirmations is this:

- Intentions are seeds I want to plant.
- *Declaring and Claiming* is digging in the soil and actually and consciously planting the seeds.
- Affirmations are watering, cultivating, and nurturing the seeds.

Your "North Star" Vision Creation Story

I define a *vision creation* as a compilation of affirmations that are compiled in a way that creates a positive energetic response within. I view it as a trade-in and upgrade from one's old victim story. It can be a list of affirmations or a narrative. You can add color, pictures, or anything you can think of that will enhance the positive energy you are consciously creating. (See *Example of a "North Star" Vision Creation Story* on the next page.)

Again, I do believe in miracles, and I want to be open and receptive to them at all times. That is why I like to include a supportive addendum at the end of my vision stories.

In many of the transformational programs, courses, and workshops I have taken since the 1980s, the following success mindset left an impression on me. Though various people state it in different ways, here is the central idea. After stating your affirmations and/or creating your vision story, add something akin to the following statement:

> *I _______________ (embrace / claim / affirm) this, or something even more _______________ (grand/magnificent/delightful), for the _______________ (greatest / maximum / highest / grandest) _______________ (benefit / blessing / outcome) for myself and others.*

Energetic Qualities of "North Star" Vision Creation Stories

- Positive / supportive / uplifting / affirming wording
- Commitment to transformation
- Openness / willingness / flexibility / adaptability
- Grounding in the here and now
- Projection of positive energy and successful outcomes into your future

Example of a "North Star" Vision Creation Story

I Am excited!

I Am experiencing an amazingly new relationship with money.

I Am experiencing money liberation and expansion. Each and every day, I Am witnessing and experiencing increasing streams of money—which I gratefully receive ...

I affirm all of this and even more—much greater and grander than what I can possibly imagine—for the maximum benefit to myself, others, and the entire planet.

Prayer = Talking to God / Spirit / Your Highest Power

Based on an informal survey I conducted, there are a myriad of reasons for talking, but the top five reasons are:

1. To be heard;
2. To express yourself;
3. To share your perspective of a story;
4. To vent; and
5. To share a grievance.

Talking does not necessarily mean that you engage in a dialogue. Talking can be a one-sided tirade, a monologue, a soliloquy.

Simply stated, I view prayer as talking *to* God / Spirit / Highest Power. Admittedly, on more than a few occasions and while in the guise of praying, I have been guilty of having my own one-sided tirades, monologues, and soliloquies directed toward God.

These forms of communication are not effective in human relationships—especially when they are the main style of conversation. I realized that they were not effective when talking to God, either. At the end of doing this form of so-called prayer, I was left feeling more frustrated and alone. This contributed to my sense of separation from the Divine.

Upon reflection, I asked myself, *Are my prayers effective? If not, why not? If yes, why?* Wanting to dissect this further, I asked myself, *What is the desired effect of prayer? Is there something I could do differently that would contribute to a more enhanced experience of praying? If yes, what makes a prayer / praying effective?*

After studying different types of prayer, I decided to experiment and change how I prayed. Below are some of the things I learned and experienced, and what I believe does contribute to a greater sense of openness and connectedness to the Divine while praying.

Energetic Qualities of Praying

- Honesty
- Openness / vulnerability
- Willingness to transform
- Affirming
- Gratitude
- Trusting God / Spirit / Highest Power
- Flexibility

Elements to Include While Praying

- Address God.
- Speak from your heart.
- Express humility (see Chapter 5 in *Getting God*® ~ "*The GOD Project*"); acknowledge God as God / Spirit / Highest Power, and express gratitude for that.
- Acknowledge openness to God's infinite wisdom and divine plan for everyone involved in the situation.
- Listen.
- Express even more gratitude.

- Affirm: Thank you. I am grateful. And so it is. Amen!
- Trust in God that the best thing for all souls involved will transpire.

Example of Effective Prayer

God / Spirit / Highest Power, I Am open and receptive to bringing forth whatever can be released and will make a significant difference with my healing and transformation at this time—including my relationship with and my experience of money. I know You are with me and guiding this process in an easy and gentle manner. I pray for deeper understanding, greater awareness, and opening up to Your loving presence in my life—including financial prosperity and *money liberation* now.

[*Now Listen...*]

Thank you for Your love and support, now and always. I affirm, *declare and claim* this—and even more delightful and joyful awareness and experiences—for my greatest benefit and for the greatest benefit of all others as well. Thank you. I Am grateful.

And so it is. Amen.

Meditation = Listening to God

Simply stated, meditation means *listening* to God / Spirit / Highest Power. It does not mean listening for what you hope to hear. Meditation is not about manipulating anything to get a specifically desired outcome. It is not meant to uphold or support your thinking mind's thoughts, stories, perceived wrongs, and other misperceptions.

Meditation is about being open and vulnerable enough to accept whatever comes forward without interference from the thinking mind. It is also about a willingness to listen for and to hear Truth (capital "T") rather than what the thinking mind / ego / human personality wants to label as truth and wants to hear. It is a time to turn within and tune into your Intuition, which I believe is the voice of God Within. It is meant to liberate you from the thinking mind and support you in connecting with the mind of God Within.

While meditation is often described in various ways, including a mindfulness practice, for those new to the concept and practice, you can view it in these ways:

- Meditation is a mind-*less*-ness practice—an opportunity to practice disconnecting from the head chattering / monkey mind / munching mind—creating stillness within to be open to not only perceiving God's / Spirit's Inner Guidance but also being able to clearly attune to it.
- Meditation is a mind-*full*-ness practice. After being able to quiet the chattering mind, it creates space in which you can connect with The Oneness—and *fill* your mind with The Mind of God / Spirit / Highest Power.

Either way, meditation is a practice—and requires practice. When I make it a habit to meditate—even for a few minutes on a regular basis, I find that my body and my psyche actually begin to crave doing it. I feel a bit off if I do not take a few minutes to simply attune inwardly and be still. The more I meditate, the more I want to meditate.

How to Begin to Meditate

Quiet your mind. Tune in to the rhythm of your heartbeat, or to the rise and fall of your chest, while you deeply inhale and exhale.

If your attention wanders and you begin to engage with your thinking mind, be gentle with yourself and simply return to the stillness within.

Optional: At the beginning of the meditation, you can state your intention to receive Inner Knowing about a specific topic. You can also ask a question, request guidance, information, support, and/or inspiration.

Energetic Qualities of Meditation

- Openness / vulnerability
- Acceptance
- Listening with an open heart and mind
- Willingness
- Humility (see Chapter 5 in *Getting God®* ~ *"The GOD Project"*)

Examples of Meditation Queries (Optional)

- What does God / Spirit / Highest Power want to reveal to me about money?
- What does money want to reveal to me about itself?
- What would it feel like if I had unlimited money?
- How can I become more open and receptive to *money liberation*?

Moving Forward

Change—any change—can be quite threatening to some people.

After releasing old and ineffective energy blocks and imbalances (both conscious and unconscious / subconscious) and incorporating new insights and ways of being within yourself (toward money, others, and to life and living in general), moving forward is the next step.

Moving forward takes courage. That is especially true when unhappy, angry, fearful, and judgmental people notice a shift in you. Some may feel threatened because your reaction to the interaction between the two of you is no longer the same or predictable. Your responses and interactions become unpredictable—and this can be quite unsettling for them. Some may want to remind you of your past in an attempt to keep you bound, captive, held hostage, and forever tethered to your past. They want to define you based on their perceptions / misperceptions / negative projections of their—and your—past. They view you through their rearview mirror.

Actually, all this does is keep *them* tethered to *their* own past—*their* own misperceptions and distortions based on *their* own inner negativity. They are trying to hoist their negative perceptions of their past into their—and your—present and future. These people want to hold on to their own past and use it as a weapon to keep you in place. That place happens to be within their own negativity, judgments, unhappiness, and fear. They think they can use that place as leverage to control you. In fact, it only serves as a means of constriction and confinement within them. It holds *them* hostage and bound to *their* past.

Others who have not yet moved forward themselves may say things such as:

- "How dare you rock the boat!"
- "I remember when you said (or did) ________."
- "You acted like ________."
- "I remember the time when you were ________."
- "I will never forget the time when you said (or did) ________."
- "I will never forgive you for ________."
- "I will never forget or forgive you for the time when you ________."

Energetic Qualities of Moving Forward

- Having determination / resolve
- Embracing fortitude / perseverance
- Loving and caring for everyone involved, including yourself
- Releasing

- Allowing
- Being nonjudgmental

Examples of Moving Forward

When confronted and challenged by those in fear, resistance, and judgment who are experiencing anger, unhappiness, and discontent within their own lives, it would behoove you to focus your energy and attention on your continuing transformation. Focus on your intentions and commitment to your growth and upliftment. In other words, "Keep on keeping on."

A more positive reframing or perceiving of others' reactive and negative responses to your evolution can be applied to the degree of others' reactions (such as anger, disturbance, reactiveness, defensiveness, and attacking). Neutrally observing the amount and/or intensity of others' negative reactions can be a great tool for you to measure how much you have grown, been uplifted, and transformed. More simply stated, the strength of others' negative reactions can reflect, proportionally, the degree to which you have transformed.

Some things to consider: Sometimes allowing and releasing may mean allowing other people to be themselves and releasing any and all judgments you may have against *them* for how they are reacting to your transformation. At times, it may mean releasing the relationship—allowing your continuing upliftment and transformation with freedom from their negative reactions, energy, repercussions, and interference.

At all times, try your utmost to be loving and caring
toward everyone—especially those who are on a
different path in life.

May ***everything*** serve as a blessing and lesson for you.

Remember, at all times, try your utmost to be grateful
for the gifts and blessings that negatively reactive
people have been in your life—
and bless them and their journeys.

Move forward on your own path—
loving them and yourself—along the way.

—Dr. Linda Humphreys

PART IV

THE ENERGETICS
OF
MONEY LIBERATION

Chapter 15

Elements of the Energetics of Money Liberation

It takes a deep commitment to change and an even deeper commitment to grow.

—***Ralph Ellison***

To keep things simple, I have distilled the *money liberation* process / project into several key theoretical and practical elements. Each of these elements is listed as a step, and the process of each step is covered in more detail in individual chapters.

Money Liberation Project Overview

When you think about money and how you perceive your relationship with money, you will want to follow these steps:

Step 1: Evaluate and Determine

In this first step, you will consider:

- how you feel / what you perceive now;
- your perceived stress or challenge level;
- what you want to experience;
- your intentions for this relationship;
- what you are willing to *declare and claim*;
- affirmations in support of your intentions, declaring, and claiming; and
- creating a vision of what you want to experience.

Step 2: Explore

Next, you will explore your:

- religious / church-based indoctrinations about money;
- family of origin indoctrinations;
- perceptions of parental figures' relationship with money; and
- perceptions of your relationship with money.

Step 3: Examine Your Thoughts and Feelings

Then you will examine your:

- judgments and resentments about others with money, others' lack of money, and your own money state;
- your shadow self (what you do not want to own about yourself—particularly as it relates to money);
- positive thoughts, feelings, and energy; and
- negative thoughts, feelings, and energy about yourself—and money.

Step 4: Expose via Divining

Now you will uncover your subconscious thoughts by:

- using the beginning session protocol for *all* sessions;
- divining which statement to clear first ... next ... next; and
- divining for more information.

Step 5: Eliminate through Energetic Clearing and Releasing

Next you will clear and release by:

- divining which energetic clearing modality to use;
- using the energetic clearing modality indicated;

- addressing negative / challenged subconscious and conscious thoughts and energy; and
- addressing energetic blocks and imbalances causing separation from positive or lack of positive subconscious and conscious thoughts and energy.

Step 6: Empower

Finally, you will empower yourself by:

- using supportive *money liberation* practices;
- continuing to study, investigate, meditate about, ask for guidance and clarity about money—and your relationship to it;
- checking in within, connecting with yourself, connecting with Spirit, and connecting with Spirit and you as a whole—to experience greater wholeness and the fullness of life—including financial prosperity; and
- getting additional support on all levels.

Additionally, it is my prayer that you *emerge* renewed and continue to use the practices and tools offered and experience:

- new energy;
- greater clarity;
- less levels of stress / challenge as it relates to your perceived relationship with money;
- improved perception and experience of financial prosperity;
- more positive experiences of love and compassion toward yourself;
- more positive experiences of compassion toward others;
- greater openness to all of the good, the blessings, the riches—metaphoric and literal—the beauty, and all the

love and magic that God / Spirit / Your Highest Power / the Universe has in store for you; and

- *money liberation*!

More detailed suggestions, examples, and additional support materials can be found in *The Energetics of Money Liberation ~ The* PLAY*book—Support for Your Money Liberation Project.*

Chapter 16

Step 1: Evaluate and Determine

Knowing yourself is the beginning of all wisdom.

—Aristotle

As with any project, experiment, and transformation endeavor, it is always good to establish a baseline in which you can measure your progress. Your *money liberation process* is no different. As part of your *Money Liberation Project*, journal your responses to the queries below.

Evaluate

Start by using the following as the baseline questions:

When you think about money and how you perceive your relationship with money

- how do you feel?
- what do you perceive now?
- what is your perceived stress or challenge level now?

Stress / Challenge Evaluation

Find a quiet time and space. Take a moment to connect to your body through deep breathing. Connect with your feelings. Silently read the questions below. Journal your responses.

On a scale of 1 to 10 (1 = ever so slightly stressed / challenged; 10 = deeply, disturbingly stressed / challenged), rate the following:

- How much of a challenge is / how much stress are you currently experiencing with your perceived relationship with money?

- When you think about the current status of your relationship with money, what amount of stress do you experience within?
- How blocked / closed off do you feel regarding receiving money?
- How blocked / closed off do you feel regarding giving money to others (individuals, organizations)?
- How much of a challenge is / how much stress are you currently experiencing regarding saving and/or keeping money?
- How much frustration do you feel regarding your relationship with money?

Add other statements or observations about your stresses and challenges.

Determine

With any project or experiment, it is always a good idea to establish what direction you want to be going in and what you are working toward.

Find a quiet time and space. Take a moment to connect to your body through deep breathing. Connect with your feelings. Silently read the question below. Journal your response.

- What do you want to experience in your relationship with money?

Mindset of Success

In many of the transformational programs, courses, and workshops I have taken since the 1980s, the following success mindset left an impression on me, and I like to incorporate it whenever possible. Though various people state it in different ways, here is the central idea:

> *If this (book, program, project) were to be ________________ (immensely, wildly, greatly) successful, what would you experience?*

Now, it is your turn. Answer the following:

If this money liberation __________________ (book, program, project, experiment) were to be __________________ (immensely, wildly, greatly) successful, I would experience __________________.

You can use these techniques to explore other parts of your *Money Liberation Project.*[6]

- **Your Intentions.** Using your responses to the last statement above can assist you in creating your intentions. Create your *money liberation* intentions now.
- **Your Declarations and Claiming.** Starting with your intentions, change them to make energy-infused *declaring and claiming* statements now.
- **Your Affirmations.** Using your intentions and *declaring and claiming* statements can assist you in creating affirmations. Create your *money liberation* affirmations now.
- **Your North Star Vision Creation Story.** Using your affirmations can assist you in your Vision Creation. Create your *money liberation* vision now.

---

[6] See Chapter 14, Energy Tools and Qualities of Transformation, and *The Energetics of Money Liberation ~ The* PLAY*book—Support for Your Money Liberation Project* for additional information and support.

Chapter 17

Step 2: Explore

When I discover who I am, I'll be free.

—Ralph Ellison

I believe it is imperative to consciously explore your memory to trace the root cause of your sense and perception of separation from money / financial prosperity. As part of your *Money Liberation Project*, you will be asked to explore what you learned about money, how you learned it, and who you learned it from. You will also be asked to journal your responses to the reflections and queries that follow.

Indoctrinations

Looking into the religion in which you were born and the belief systems (dogmas / indoctrinations / programs) that were instilled in you as you were growing up is the good place to start when exploring your sense of separation.

Religion / Church Indoctrination. In the books, songs, and movies you were exposed to in your religion, church, affiliated events and gatherings, catechism, and Saturday or Sunday school, how was money and/or how were rich people described? How were you, in relationship to money, described?

Family of Origin Indoctrination. If your mother was present during your upbringing, how would you describe her relationship with money? What did she say about money? Rich people? Other people and money? (If your mother was not present, how did the most influential female figure during your upbringing relate to money? What did she say about money?)

If your father was present during your upbringing, how would you describe his relationship with money? What did he say about money? Rich people? Other people and money? (If your father was not present, how did the most influential male figure during your upbringing, relate to money? What did he say about money?)

Perceptions of Relationships with Money

The ways your parental influences related with money—and your perceptions of their relationships with money—affected your perception of your own relationship with money.

Perceptions of Parental Figures' Relationships with Money. If you were to describe the relationship your mother or the most influential female in your life had with money—based purely on your perspective and perceptions—how would you describe it?

If you were to describe the relationship your father or the most influential male in your life had with money—based purely on your perspective and perceptions—how would you describe it?

Perceptions of Your Relationship with Money. If you were to describe your relationship with money while you were growing up—based purely on your perspective and perceptions—how would you describe it?

Today, if you were to describe your relationship with money—based purely on your perspective and perceptions—how would you describe it?

Looking back, did your relationship with money reflect your relationship with your most challenging parental figure?

Challenging Characteristics and Relationships with Money

Challenging relationship characteristics—even regarding money—can be serially repeated and experienced. Explore the challenging common denominator(s) within your relationships.

Challenging Parental Figure. Which relationship did you find to be more challenging while you were growing up: the relationship with your mother (or an influential female figure) or with your father (or an influential male figure)? How would you describe the characteristics of the person you were more challenged by?

I believe there is a correlation between our negative perceptions / misperceptions of our most influential parental figures, of money, and ourselves. The order in which these appeared in your conscious and/or subconscious does not actually matter. Regardless of the order, they produce a looping effect: as one aspect is affected, so are the others.

BOTTOM LINE: For a clearer, healthier, more accurate, and more positive perception of your relationship with money to manifest, whatever is muddled, unhealthy, inaccurate, imbalanced, challenging, and negative must be identified and removed.

Chapter 18

Step 3: Examine Your Thoughts and Feelings

The unexamined life is not worth living.

—Socrates

Although you are not your story, within your story resides aspects of you that need to be addressed and energetically released and cleared so you can transform and spiritually evolve. In this step, you will examine thoughts and feelings that contributed to the creation and perpetuation of your story of you and of your relationship with money.

Using paper separate from your journal (because these pages will be shredded after your clearings), write what comes forward for you as you read through the following ideas. Go within, and be as honest as possible.

Judgments and Resentments

Consider the following: *What judgments and resentments do you hold against your most challenging parent / influential person? Against others because of their wealth—or lack of it? Yourself?*

Relationship Mirrors and Projections

I have observed that relationships can act as mirrors of both conscious and subconscious feelings as well as attitudes, beliefs, perceptions, and misperceptions. Quite often, what we do not want to accept in ourselves, we project (or place) onto others—especially if we deem the things we do not want to accept as negative.

This is not a new concept. It is a basic principle of psychology. (I learned this in Psychology 101.) I have, however, experienced and witnessed it firsthand—specifically and directly as it relates to perceptions and misperceptions of a myriad of things—including money.

What Do You Not Want to Own about Yourself—as It Relates to Money?

Holding the mirror up to yourself can assist in acknowledging and owning your shadow side. It is a vital step in your transformational process.

This step requires rigorous honesty. By bringing light to your shadow side, it helps clear negative energy and paves the way for you to, subsequently, acknowledge and own your own Inner Divinity—and birthright as a Child of the Divine. Continue to journal your responses to the following questions on separate paper.

As it relates to all aspects of you and money (for example: spending, saving, giving to others, and so on ...),

- *what do you perceive are aspects of your shadow side—the part of your personality you judge as bad, wrong, and/or unacceptable?*
- *what are you hoping is not true of your personality (yet most likely is)? Specifically, what are you hoping is not true of your money personality?*
- *what personality characteristics are you most ashamed of?*
- *if someone were to describe your personality—particularly regarding you and money—what terms would trigger a defensive response within you?*

Plus ... again, as it relates to you and money,

- *what do you perceive are aspects of your positive side, the part of your personality you judge as "not me"—and too good to be true?*
- *what are you hoping is true of your personality—and how you relate to money?*

- *what money-related personality characteristics are you most proud of, but fear they are not actually true?*
- *if someone were to describe your personality—particularly regarding you and money—what positive terms would trigger a defensive response within you?*

Positive and Negative Aspects

I believe a holistic approach to removing blocks and imbalances in the conscious and subconscious mind involves addressing the presence of Negative / Challenged Statement energetics, programs, and vibrations, *plus* the Lack of Positive statement energetics, programs, and vibrations. I assert that both—the presence of a negative *plus* the absence of a positive—are equally detrimental. Equal attention must be placed on the exploration, release, and clearing of *both* the presence of negative energy and the absence of positive energy.

Exploration Statements

In this book and the accompanying *The Energetics of Money Liberation: The* PLAY*book—Support for Your Money Liberation Project*, I provide statements you can use as a springboard and catalyst for the creation of your own statements. As statements occur to you, write them down.

The lists I have provided are not all-inclusive and are not in any specific order or hierarchy. They are merely samplings. Sources of additional statements include:

- what you journaled about during the Explore and Examine segments of the process (see Chapters 17 and 18);
- what you want to be true;
- what you fear is true;
- what you fear is not true; and
- whatever thought about money / finances that stirs emotion within you (both positive and negative / challenging).

The number of statements and the exact statements that need to be cleared vary for each individual. As more layers are revealed and cleared, even more statements and corresponding energetic vibrations may be revealed. As I stated earlier, our perceived challenges can have multiple layers—like an onion—that need to be peeled away one layer at a time. This is also akin to removing the prickly leaves of an artichoke to reveal the soft heart within.

To get the most transformative value out of this process, it is best to be vulnerable, open, and honest with yourself. There is no judgment—so go for the greatest amount and level of clearing, releasing, and transformation possible for you at this time.

Remember ... This is not a mental / thinking discernment process. This is not a processing of any story. This is not a processing process. It is a process of trusting what is energetically identified by using energy-identifying tools. If you want to use a mind, allow your God Mind—your Divine Mind—to lead this process.

Sample Statements

We impose and infuse energy and vibrations onto words. In this transformational context, and as in all areas of life, words do matter.

While some of the statements and concepts listed in the sample statements may seem redundant, there are reasons why certain concepts are separated and distinguished. To illustrate this, consider the following statements:

- I am ready to accept *money liberation—now*!
- I am willing to accept *money liberation—now*!
- I am able to accept *money liberation—now*!

Though your thinking mind may rationalize that *ready*, *willing*, and *able* are synonymous—the thinking mind tends to compartmentalize things. Your thinking mind can identify ready and willing and able as three separate things and distinct things and rationalize reasons for doing so. This compartmentalization leads to the creation of three (or more) separate and distinct layers. It is important to realize that each word carries specific vibrations.

Additionally, in combination statements such as "I am open and receptive to receiving money—*now*!" the combination of the words and vibrations of "open" plus "receptive" plus "*now*!" carries a different and distinct vibration separate and apart from segregated individual statement components.

When you create your statements, do not censor yourself. Write whatever comes forward and into your awareness. If you have an exact replication of a specific statement, you can delete the exact repetitive statement. Having said that, if you find yourself consistently repeating a specific statement, it is most likely an indication that the specific statement and its vibration are what want and need to be addressed—perhaps even first. You can verify all of this through divining (see Chapter 19).

Divining Statements

In the following charts, I have provided some sample Lack of Positive Statements and Negative / Challenged Statements. In addition to what you create for yourself, you will find many more statements, assistive formatting, and some additional information in *The Energetics of Money Liberation: The* PLAY*book—Support for Your Money Liberation Project.*

Statement Lists Format

The format of the statements lists was designed to support easy tracking of the statements. There is no particular statement hierarchy, order, or grouping. Each chart page has the following:

- Type of Statement (Lack of Positive or Negative / Challenged)
- Page number
- Fifteen statements broken down into three groups (A, B, C)

of five statements (1 through 5) for easy tracking

- A place to note when you were Challenged as indicated via divining
  - If you test *weak* or *no* regarding a positive statement on a Lack of Positive Statements chart
  - If you test *strong* or *yes* regarding a negative statement on a Negative / Challenged Statements chart
  - If you test *strong* or *yes* for needing to know more information about the energetic
- A place to note the energetic was cleared and released

What You Will Be Tracking

During your *Money Liberation Project*, you will be tracking which energetic statement best represents your Challenged energetic blocks and imbalances—and those that are not a challenge *plus* statement energetics that indicate you need to know more information. You will also be tracking the energetic clearing and release.

How to Manage and Track Your Divining Statements

There are different types of Challenged energetics: lack of positive energetics and negative energetics. It is imperative that both be addressed.

Lack of Positive Statements

- While divining, if you get a *strong* or *yes* response, you can leave the *Challenged* box clear or mark the box with a 0. (I left the box blank because it was easier for me to clearly spot the boxes that were checked.) These statements contain the subconscious / unconscious and conscious thoughts, energy, and vibration that resonate as what you hold as *True*.

- If you get a *weak* or *no* response, mark the *Challenged* box with a check. These statements represent energetic dissonance and what you hold within your subconscious / unconscious and conscious thoughts, energy, and vibration as *False* or *Not True*.

Negative / Challenged Statements

- While divining, if you get a *weak* or *no* response, mark the box with a 0. These statements contain the subconscious / unconscious and conscious thoughts, energy, and vibration that resonate as what you hold as *False* or *Not True*.
- If you get a *strong* or *yes* response, mark the *Challenged* box with a check. These statements contain the subconscious / unconscious and conscious thoughts, energy, and vibration that resonate as what you hold as *True*.

Need to Know More Information (Any Statement)

There may be times you are directed, via divining, to need more information. This is how to track that:

- While divining, if you get a *strong* or *yes* response after inquiring if you need to know more information, within the *Challenged* box either add an "I," circle the check, or create your own notation.

Clearing and Releasing

In Chapter 18, you will learn how to clear and release energetic blocks and imbalances.

Lack of Positive Statements

- When a Lack of Positive Statement energetic clearing and release has taken place, it means that the energetic block and/or imbalance toward resonance with the positive statement and associated energy has been removed.

Negative / Challenged Statements

- When a Negative / Challenged Statements energetic clearing and release has taken place, it means that whatever negative energetic block and/or imbalance which created resonance with the Negative / Challenged Statement within your subconscious / unconscious and/or energy field has been cleared.
- Within the *Cleared* box, you can either write the date it was cleared, check the box indicating a clearing, or write a "C."

NOTE: Though the statements within the Lack of Positive Statements chart are *positive* statements, the intention is to test and track which positive statement energetic is *lacking* or *absent* from one's energy field and/or subconscious.

Lack of Positive Statements (Page 1)	Challenged	Info	Cleared
GROUP A			
1. Money gravitates to me.			
2. I am a good steward of money.			
3. I am worthy of receiving all that is good—including money.			
4. Money is good.			
5. I deserve to have money.			
GROUP B			
1. Being rich and wealthy is part of my destiny.			
2. I give myself permission to be wealthy.			
3. I am ready to accept money liberation—now!			
4. I am willing to accept money liberation—now!			
5. I am able to accept money liberation—now!			
GROUP C			
1. Money is always there for me.			
2. I trust myself with handling money.			
3. I am excited about all of the good I can do with my money.			
4. When I think about my finances, I feel calm.			
5. I am comfortable with having a vast sum of money.			

Negative / Challenged Statements (Page 1)	Challenged	Info	Cleared
GROUP A			
1. Money is never there for me.			
2. Having no money is God's way of testing me.			
3. I am being punished—and that is why I don't have any money.			
4. No matter how hard I try, money is elusive to me.			
5. I have bad luck with money.			
GROUP B			
1. It is my lot in life to not be rich.			
2. Wealthy people are bad.			
3. It is bad to be wealthy			
4. Doing something immoral and/or illegal is the only way to become rich.			
5. God wants me to suffer—and having no money is part of my suffering.			
GROUP C			
1. I have to work hard to earn money.			
2. Only the rich and wealthy get richer and wealthier.			
3. No matter how hard I work, I can never get ahead financially.			
4. Because I was not born wealthy, I will never become wealthy.			
5. God is withholding money from me.			

Chapter 19

Step 4: Expose via Divining

Until you make the unconscious conscious, it will direct your life and you will call it fate.

—***Carl Jung***

Divining your way into your subconscious / unconscious is intended to be a process that is gentle, supportive, and guided by God / Spirit / Highest Power. It is a way to connect the aspect of God Within to that of God Throughout. There are check-ins after each and every step along the way—to make sure you can proceed without any major disturbing upheaval—on any and all levels. It is important to follow the detailed protocols to make sure this is not, in any way, a disruptive process.

Again, like a lie detector, divining assists in discovering and discerning truth / resonance and falsehood / dissonance. Divining is also a tool that can be used to discover and discern energetic blocks and imbalances that are present within your subconscious / unconscious and your energy field.

A Friendly Suggestion

Though not a requirement, meditation is an essential tool to utilize and incorporate into one's spiritual tool kit. I have found that meditating—either before or after a clearing and release session—has been extremely beneficial for me.

Two Ways to Divine

There are numerous methods for divining, and you will find many explained in *The Energetics of Money Liberation ~ The* PLAY*book—Support for Your Money Liberation Project.*

Here, though, I will share one that requires two people and another method that you can do by yourself. Each method includes some adaptations and options.

Before beginning any step,

1. stop if you meet resistance;
2. continue when ready; and
3. always stop if you meet any resistance at any stage.

Two-Person Divining: Outstretched Arm Test (Standing or Sitting)

Begin by having the test taker (testee) outstretch either arm to the side of his or her body.

Tester:

- Set your intention to clearly and easily establish the testee's *strong* (or *yes*) and *weak* (or *no*) baselines. (See below.)
- If testee is standing, stand in front of the testee's raised arm; if testee is seated, sit in a chair in front of the testee's raised arm.
    - You can also stand behind the testee.
    - Whichever you choose, continue testing consistently using the same procedures throughout.
- Place one hand on the shoulder of the side of the testee's outstretched arm; the other hand should be on the testee's outstretched forearm.
- While divining, do not exert brute force. Lightly apply pressure on the testee's forearm. (This is not a test of anyone's physical force, willpower, and/or resistance strength.)

Testee:

- Set your intention to clearly and easily establish your *strong* (or *yes*) and *weak* (or *no*) baselines.
- Do not exert tense resistance. Use mild resistance. (Again, this is not a test of anyone's willpower, physical strength, and/or resistance strength.)

How to Establish Your Baselines

As previously stated, establishing baselines is an essential process for each and every divining session—and also the first things that must be discerned. With each method, how a *strong / yes* and *weak / no* will feel and look like will be provided.

A. Establish a Clear Strong or Yes Baseline (Two-Person: Outstretched Arm)

Goal / Intention: To get a clear *strong / yes* without muscle strain, force, and so on. While divining, the arm's position should remain *strong* after stating something that is *true*.

- **Testee:** With an outstretched arm, say something that is true while maintaining mild resistance. For example:

  My name is ______________.
- **Tester:** Lightly apply pressure on the testee's outstretched forearm.
- **Testee:** Continue to maintain mild resistance.

Baseline Response: Strong or Yes (Two-Person: Outstretched Arm)

- Via divining, if:
  - while testee states something *truthful*; and
  - *simultaneously uses mild resistance*;
  - while the tester uses gentle pressure on testee's forearm—
  - and the testee's arm position remains *strong* and does not release—

- this would indicate a *yes = truthful / congruent* statement.

The tester and testee can now discern what the testee's *yes / affirmative / congruent* divining baseline response looks like and feels like.

Continuation Procedures

- Tester and Testee: Divine if you can proceed.
  - If testee's arm position remains *strong* (*yes*), continue.
  - If testee's arm position becomes *weak* (*no*), refer to *What to Do if You Get a No (Weak) to Proceed* on page 107–108.

NOTE: If testee's arm position becomes *weak* (or *no*) when testing a true statement—stop! Refer to *What to Do if You Are Not Able to Discern Your Yes and No* on page 107.

B. Establish a Clear Weak or No Baseline (Two-Person: Outstretched Arm)

Goal / Intention: To get a clear *weak* or *no* without muscle strain, force, and so on. While divining, the arm's hold should become *weak* and essentially collapse its position after stating something *false*.

- **Testee:** With an outstretched arm, say something that is not true while maintaining mild resistance. For example:

  My name is ____________. (State a false name.)

- **Tester:** Lightly apply pressure on the testee's outstretched forearm.
- **Testee:** Continue to maintain mild resistance.

Baseline Response: Weak or No (Two-Person: Outstretched Arm)

- If the testee's arm position becomes *weak* and does not remain strong—this would indicate a *no = not truthful / incongruent* statement.

The tester and testee have now established what the testee's *no / not affirmative / incongruent* divining baseline looks like and feels like.

Continuation Procedures

- Tester and Testee: Divine if you can proceed.
    - If testee's arm position remains *strong* (*yes*), continue.
    - If testee's arm position becomes *weak* (*no*), refer to *What to Do if You Get a No (Weak) to Proceed* on page 107–108.

NOTE: If testee's arm position becomes *weak* (or *no*) when testing a true statement—stop! Refer to *What to Do if You Are Not Able to Discern Your Yes and No* on page 107.

Divining by Yourself: Interlocking Fingers

Begin by interlocking your pinkie fingers together. Actually, you can do this with any of your fingers—except for the thumbs. Additionally, you can form interlocking rings with your fingers by interlocking either middle finger and thumbs or index fingers and thumbs.

A. Establish a Clear Strong or Yes Baseline (Interlocking Fingers)

Goal / Intention: To get a clear *strong* or *yes* without muscle strain, force, and so on. The fingers should maintain their locked hold with mild resistance.

- Set your intention to clearly and easily establish your *strong / yes / congruent* baseline.
- With fingers interlocked, maintain mild resistance while saying something that is true—while gently trying to break the hold of the interlocked fingers. For example:

My name is ______________.

- Apply gentle pressure to interlocked fingers while maintaining mild resistance.
- Via divining, if—while stating something *truthful*—the hold / link of your interlocking fingers remains *strong* and does not break / release with mild resistance and gentle pressure, this would indicate a *yes = truthful / congruent* statement.
    - You can now discern what your *yes / affirmative / congruent* divining response baseline response looks like and feels like.
- Divine if you can proceed.
- If you test *strong* or *yes*, continue.
    - If you test *weak* or *no*, refer to *What to Do if You Get a No (Weak) to Proceed* on page 107–108.
- If you get a *weak* or *no* response when testing the truthful statement—stop!
    - Refer to *What to Do if You Are Not Able to Discern Your Yes and No* on page 107.

B. Establish a Clear Weak or No Baseline (Interlocking Fingers)

Goal / Intention: To get a clear *weak* or *no* without muscle strain, force, and so on. The fingers should break their locked hold with gentle pressure and mild resistance.

- With fingers interlocked, maintain mild resistance while saying something that is not true—while gently trying to break the hold of the interlocked fingers. For example:

  My name is ______________. (State a false name.)

- Via divining, if—while stating something *not truthful*—the hold / link of your interlocking fingers becomes *weak* and breaks / releases with mild resistance and gentle pressure, this would indicate a *no = not truthful / incongruent* statement.

  - You have now established what your *no / not affirmative / incongruent* divining baseline looks like and feels like.
  - Via divining, you can now discern between *yes / truthful / congruent* and *no / not truthful / incongruent* responses.
- Next, divine whether or not you can continue at this time.
  - If you test *strong* or *yes*, continue.
  - If you test *weak* or *no*, refer to *What to Do if You Get a No (Weak) to Proceed* on page 107–108.
- Next, if you are not able to discern between your *yes* and *no*—stop!
  - Refer to *What to Do if You Are Not Able to Discern Your Yes and No* on page 107.

After a clear baseline has been established, you can begin testing anything (food, supplement, statement, idea) to see if it is ***energetically*** congruent / beneficial / present (as it relates to statements) for you and your energy system and presents a *strong* or *yes* response. Additionally, you can decipher whether something is ***energetically*** incongruent / not beneficial / not present (as it relates to statements) for you and your energy system, resulting in a *weak* or *no* response.

Summary of Divining Steps with Protocols

Below you will find all of the recommended steps and protocols that will assist you with the divining process during your *Money Liberation Project.*

Beginning Session Protocol for All Divining Sessions

For this to be a process of ease and gentleness, it is imperative to establish and adhere to certain protocols.

- Invoke God / Spirit / Highest Power and say a heartfelt prayer.

- State your energetic clearing and releasing intention (verbally or silently).
    - For example: It is my intention to partner with God / Spirit / Highest Power and to clearly discern which statement needs / wants to be cleared and released at this time.
- Discern which divining / AK / muscle testing[7] to use by using your intuition.
- Establish your baselines.

Establish Your Baselines (All Divining Sessions)

- State your intention to discern, with ease and clarity, your divining baselines.
- Establish your *strong / yes / congruent* baseline.
    - State something that is *true / factual*. Divine.
    - If you test *strong* or *yes*,
        - you have established what your *yes / true / congruent* statement looks like and feels like while divining.
- If you get a *no* when testing the *true / factual* statement—stop!
    - Refer to *What to Do if You Are Not Able to Discern Your Yes and No* (see below).
    - Establish your *weak / no / incongruent* baseline.
    - State something that is *not true*. Divine.
    - If you test *weak* or *no* regarding this *not truthful* statement,
        - you have established your *no / false / incongruent* baseline; and
        - you can now discern how your *yes* and *no* feels like and looks like when divining.
    - If you are not able to discern between your *yes* and *no*—stop!

[7] From now on, I will only use the word *divine* or *divining*.

    - Refer to *What to Do if You Are Not Able to Discern Your Yes and No* (see below).

What to Do if You Are Not Able to Discern Your Yes and No

- Drink water. Wait a few minutes and try again.
- Set your intention to experience clarity with discerning *yes* and *no* while divining, in service to your growth, healing, and upliftment.
- This time, think or say out loud: "Yes! Yes! Yes! Yes!" Test for a *yes* baseline. Confirm by stating a true statement. You should experience the same baseline results.
- Now think or say out loud: "No! No! No! No!" Test for a *no* baseline. Confirm by stating a false statement. You should experience the same baseline results.
- Practice, and be patient with yourself.

Divining Continuation Protocol

- Divine if you can proceed.
    - If you test *strong* or *yes*, continue.
    - Ask if you are able to release something at this time. Divine.
        - If you get a *yes* (*strong*), proceed.
        - If you get a *no* (*weak*)—stop![8]
    - Refer to *What to Do if You Get a No (Weak) to Proceed* (see below).

What to Do if You Get a No (Weak) to Proceed

- Drink a glass of water.
- After waiting a few minutes, try again.
    - If you still get a *no* (*weak*), try again another day.

---

[8] From now on, if after getting repeated *no* (*weak*) responses to: your correct name when attempting to establish your baseline, whether to proceed, or that a clearing took place—stop. Follow the steps in *What to Do if You Get a No (Weak) to Proceed.*

  - Do not continue until you get a *yes* (*strong*) response.
- Additionally, consider:
  - going within;
  - praying for clarity and for assistance from God / Spirit / Highest Power;
  - restating your healing intention;
  - being patient and gentle with yourself; and
  - persisting ... another day.

Divining Which Statement to Clear First ... Next ... Next ...

Using divining, discern which statement to energetically address, clear, and release first, next, and so on.

Divining Statements Protocol

- Follow the ***Beginning Session Protocol for All Divining Sessions.***
- Referring to the statement charts in Chapter 18, ask God / Spirit / Highest Power which type of statement to clear first and discern via divining:
  - Lack of Positive Statements: Y / N?
  - Negative / Challenged Statements: Y / N?
- Within the category indicated, ask God / Spirit / Highest Power which of the following to clear first and discern via divining:
  - Group: A (Y / N?), B (Y / N?), C (Y / N?)
  - Number: 1? (Y / N?), 2? (Y / N?), 3? (Y / N?), 4? (Y / N?), 5? (Y / N?)
- Check the *Challenged* box corresponding to the statement indicated.
- Divine to see if more information is needed (see *Divining for More Information* and *Divining for More Information Protocol* on pages 109–111.

  - Reminder: If you are prompted to divine for more information and if there is an indication that the energetic statement was inherited, you can choose to do one of the following within the statement's *Challenged* box:
    - Circle the check.
    - Place an asterisk or the initial "I" next to the check.
    - Create a way to designate the statement as inherited within the *Challenged* box.
- If, after divining, you are given a go-ahead to proceed, begin Step 5 (next chapter).

NOTE: Within one divining statements session, you may move back and forth between both Negative / Challenged and Lack of Positive statements.

- Be patient with yourself and your process.
- See *The Energetics of Money Liberation ~ The* PLAY*book—Support for Your Money Liberation Project* for specific examples and session suggestions.

Divining for More Information

Sometimes during my own *Money Liberation Project,* I intuitively sensed I needed to know more about the origin of or experience that caused the block and/or imbalance.

Too Much Information or Need to Know?

There were other times that, although I may have been curious about the details that surrounded a block and/or imbalance, no additional information was indicated or required for me (and subsequently for my clients) to know in order for the clearing and releasing to take place.

I believe this is the reason: Some people may be quite "head-y." (At times, I tend to be very immersed within my own head.) Some may still want to be attached to their victim story. Their thinking / ego mind wants a bone to chew on; this "munching mind" wants something to gnaw on. Many times, when I ask God / Spirit / Highest Power if I (or my clients) need to know any additional or detailed information, I receive a *no* when divining.

I view receiving a *no* as a directive from God / Spirit / Highest Power to allow for an easy and gentle rebalancing. I believe that if someone is predisposed to negative perseverations and ruminations of the explicit details of their victim story, getting a *no* regarding needing to know more information is Spirit's way of swaying them from mentally picking at any former wounds—which would only reactivate the energetic vibration. It allows for whatever was cleared and released to remain cleared and released—and this supports the transformational process.

Divining for More Information Protocol

- Ask: *Do I need to know more information about this (in the context of the statement you are focusing on) at this time?* Divine.
- If you receive a *no* response about needing to know additional information, proceed to the protocols for the clearing modality indicated.
- If you receive a *yes* response, ask something like:
    - *What information do I need to know at this time?*
    - Use your intuition to be open to information to appear to you in the form of signs, symbols, words, colors, sounds, the experience of emotions, and so on.
- Ask if the issue was inherited. If you get a *yes*:
    - Ask: *What additional information do I need to know at this time?* For example: maternal or paternal side? Male or female?
    - Use your intuition to be open to information to appear to you in the form of signs, symbols, words, colors, sounds, the experience of emotions, and so on.

- Make a notation on the chart's *Challenged* box of an inherited energetic.

Chapter 20

Step 5: Eliminate
Energetic Clearing and Releasing

Becoming who you were created to be is an inside job.

—Dr. Linda Humphreys

I believe that God / Spirit / Highest Power offers us an abundance of tools with which to liberate ourselves from our inner prison of negative subconscious (and sometimes conscious) thoughts, energy, and vibrations that can cause energetic blocks and imbalances in all areas of our lives. Set your intention to heal, use your divining skills, and allow the Divine to assist with your energetic clearings and releasings, God Mind consciousness expansion, and spiritual upliftment—and now—*money liberation.*

What's Next

Now that you have uncovered specific statements / thoughts / energy / vibrations that are in your subconscious—and, perhaps, your conscious—*and* your energy field, it is time for you to release these energetic blocks / imbalances / vibrations. This step addresses how to go about doing that.

I used specific modalities that I found extremely effective in releasing energetic blocks and imbalances with my own *Money Liberation Project*. Over the years I have studied numerous subconscious / unconscious, emotional, and energetic clearing and releasing modalities. I have even become certified in several methods. Additionally, I have been inspired to create additional techniques and protocols.

I will share two modalities in this chapter. The first is what I call the *Brow, Crown, and Down* method; the second I call the

Acu-Points Rub / Tap method. Neither is superior to the other; they are just the two that have worked for me and were easy for my clients to learn. For your *Money Liberation Project*, you discern which clearing and releasing modality resonates with you.

NOTE: There may be some emotional energy releases (tears, crying, laughing) during the clearing and release process. If this should happen, it simply means that e-motion (energy in motion) is occurring.[9] During my own *Money Liberation Project*, sometimes I experienced dreamlike images and intuitive impressions, felt the energy of certain emotions, experienced sounds and colors, and received inner messages. Other times, I did not notice experiencing any of the above.

Divining Which Clearing Modality to Use Protocol (detailed)

- Use divining to discern which clearing and releasing modality would be best for you to use at this time.
    - *Brow, Crown, and Down*? (Y / N?)
    - *Acu-Points Rub / Tap*? (Y / N?)
    - **NOTE:** If you test *no* (*weak*) for both, discern which other modality (for example, one you may be familiar with and have experience with) to use by using your intuition and divining.
- After receiving the indication of which modality to use at this time, ask:
    - *Is it safe and supportive for me to continue at this time?* Divine.
    - If *yes*, continue. If you get a *no*—stop!
- Refer to *What to Do if You Get a No (Weak) to Proceed* on pages 107–108.

[9] If you do not experience a noticeable emotional release, it does not mean that a clearing and release did not occur. You can always verify a clearing through divining.

Brow, Crown, and Down

This is the modality to use if, via divining, you tested *yes* (*strong*) regarding the *Brow, Crown, and Down* clearing and releasing modality.

Tools

Both your fingertips and a magnet emit and carry electromagnetic energy, so your tools consist of:

- Your fingertips
- Optional: magnet (This can be a refrigerator magnet.)

Energy Clearing and Release Protocol for All Sessions

- Follow the ***Beginning Session Protocol for All Divining Sessions.***
- Follow ***Divining Statements Protocol.***
- Follow ***Divining for More Information Protocol.***
- Follow ***Divining Which Clearing Modality to Use Protocol.***
- If the ***Brow, Crown, and Down*** method is indicated, proceed.

Energetic Clearing and Release Procedures for a Negative / Challenged Statement[10]

This is the procedure to use if, when divining, you test *strong* (*yes*) regarding a Negative / Challenged Statement. (This indicates there is resonance between you and the Negative / Challenged energetic.)

- Using your fingertip(s), begin by either lightly rubbing in a circle (for a few seconds—approximately five to six small circles) or tapping (approximately five to six times) on the third eye area (area between eyebrows and in the center of the forehead). Proceed rubbing or tapping at various spots

[10] If the statement energetic is inherited, refer to *Clearing and Releasing Inherited Energy Protocol for All Statements (Brow, Crown, and Down)* on pages 115–116.

along the meridian line up to your crown (top of the head) and down (the back of your head to behind your neck). Rub or tap along the path described.

- Modifications:
  - Sweep your fingertips along the Brow, Crown, and Down meridian pathway instead of rubbing or tapping. Sweep several times. (I tend to sweep five or six times.)
  - Sweep the magnet instead of rubbing or tapping. Sweep several times.

- At the same time, state (verbally or silently) one or more of the following statements:
  - "Release. Release. Release."
  - "Be gone. Be gone. Be gone."
  - "I Am free! I Am free! I Am free!"
  - Or create something to that effect.

NOTE: For me, either lightly rubbing about three to six circles, tapping three to six times per point along the meridian path, or swiping the magnet or fingertips three to six times along the meridian path is sufficient most of the time; other times it takes more than six times. When uncertain, I divine to discern how many circular rubs / taps / swipes are best. It may vary from time to time. Follow your intuition.

Clearing and Releasing Inherited Energy Protocol for All Statements (Brow, Crown, and Down Method)

If there is an indication for you to divine for more information and there is an indication that the energy / vibration was inherited,

- Send a blessing to your ancestor while simultaneously doing more Brow, Crown, and Down rubs / taps / sweeps—more times than you usually would—and the amount you are intuitively guided to do and/or the amount you discern via divining.

- Additionally, rub or tap more acu-points along the meridian path.
  - Visualize a cord being untied, a chain broken, a lock opening between you and your ancestor as it relates to that specific statement—or whatever image comes forward for you.
  - You can also state things like:
    - "Release and go in peace."
    - "I honor and bless you. Be at peace. Now release."
    - Or whatever you feel your intuition is guiding you to state.

Confirm the Energetic Clearing and Release

- Ask: *Has this been released?* Divine.
- If you get a *strong* (*yes*) response, confirm the release.

How to Confirm the Release of a Negative / Challenged Statement Energetic Protocol

- Say the statement (either verbally or silently) and then divine again.
  - You should test *weak* (*no*).
- If you test *weak* (*no*) to the Negative / Challenged Statement,
  - Ask: *Is it safe and supportive for me to continue at this time?* Divine.
  - If you get a *strong* (*yes*) response, continue.

NOTE: If you still get a *strong* (*yes*) response to the Negative / Challenged Statement—stop!

- Ask: *Is it safe and supportive for me to continue at this time?* Divine.
- If you get a *strong* (*yes*) response,
  - Restate your intention to release the Negative / Challenged energetic.
  - Rub, tap, or sweep more times.

    - Remember: If this was an inherited energetic, the clearing and releasing will require more rubs / taps / swipes.
  - Say the statement (either verbally or silently) and then divine again.
    - You should test *weak* (*no*).

Another NOTE: If you still test *strong* (*yes*) for the Negative / Challenged Statement energetic or get a *weak* (*no*) response after asking if it is safe and supportive to continue at this time, follow the same protocols explained in *What to Do if You Get a No (Weak) to Proceed* on page 107–108.)

Energetic Clearing and Release Procedures for a Lack of Positive Statement[11]

This is the procedure to use if, when divining, you test *weak (no)* regarding a positive (Lack of Positive) statement using the *Brow, Crown, and Down* method. (This indicates there is dissonance / non-resonance between you and the positive energetic.)

- While rubbing or tapping on each meridian point, say (verbally or silently)—following your intuition / Inner Guidance regarding which statement to say, when to say it, and so on—one or all of the following statements:
  - "It is safe for me to experience ___________."
    Example: "It is safe for me to experience receiving money."
  - "I welcome the energy of ___________ now."
    Example: "I welcome the energy of experiencing financial wealth and *money liberation* now."
  - "It is for my maximum benefit to accept and experience ___________ now."
    Example: "It is for my maximum benefit to accept and experience receiving great sums of money now."

[11] If the statement energetic is inherited, refer to *Clearing and Releasing Inherited Energy Protocol for All Statements (Brow, Crown, and Down)* on pages 107–108.

  - And/or whatever else you feel, intuitively, that you want to state.
- Also, you can specifically address the blocks and/or imbalances:
  - "It is safe for me to remove all blocks and imbalances toward experiencing ________ now."
  - And/or something similar. Follow your intuition.

Confirm the Clearing and Release

- Ask: *Has this been released?* Divine.
- If you get a *strong* (*yes*) response, confirm the release.

How to Confirm the Release of a Lack of Positive Statement Energetic Protocol

- Say the statement (either verbally or silently) and then divine again.
- You should test *strong* (*yes*) for the positive statement energetic.
- If you test *strong* (*yes*) to the statement,
  - Ask: *Is it safe and supportive for me to continue at this time?* Divine.
  - If you get a *strong* (*yes*) response, continue.

NOTE: If you still get a *weak* (*no*) response to the positive statement—stop!

  - Ask: *Is it safe and supportive for me to continue at this time?* Divine.
  - If you get a *strong* (*yes*) response,
    - Restate your intention to release the Lack of Positive energetic.
      - Remember: If the statement's energetic / vibration is inherited, refer to *Clearing and Releasing Inherited Energy Protocol for All Statements (Brow, Crown, and Down Method).* (See pages 115-116.)

- Say the statement (either verbally or silently) and then divine again.
- You should get a *strong* (*yes*) response.

Another NOTE: If you still test *weak* (*no*) for the positive statement energetic or get a *weak* (*no*) response after asking if it is safe and supportive to continue at this time, refer to *What to Do if You Get a No (Weak) to Proceed.* (See pages 107–108.)

Always remember: Be gentle and patient with yourself. Drink lots of water. Try again another day.

Acu-Points Rub / Tap Method

Releasing energy via acu-points takes many different forms, and each form does things in slightly different ways. Some of the formal systems using tapping on acu-points are Thought Field Therapy (TFT), Tapas Acupressure Technique (TAT), and Emotional Freedom Technique (EFT).

Just as acupuncture and acupressure redirect energy via the meridian channels, so does lightly rubbing in a circular motion and/or tapping on various meridian channel points / acu-points. Though each tapping technique varies in the number of tapping points and the phrasing of release statements, all involve tapping specific points on the body.

For myself and with my clients, via divining I discern which statements need to be addressed. Next, if the *Acu-Points Rub / Tap* method is indicated as the clearing and release modality best suited at the time of testing, these are the steps I follow:

Tools

- Fingertips
- Awareness of some meridian acu-points: (partial listing)
    - Top of the head (crown)
    - "Third eye" area (center forehead above eyebrows)
    - Temple / next to the eye

- Under the eye
- Under the nose / above the lip
- Under the ear
- Middle of the chin
- Below the collarbone / below where the collarbone sticks out
- Front side of armpits
- Sides of rib cage
- Side of palm (below index finger)
- Web between index finger and thumb
- Wrist (hug with opposite hand)

NOTE: Not all of these acu-points need to be rubbed in a circular motion or tapped. Additionally, other points can be rubbed or tapped. First, practice doing all of them. Some systems use more, some use less. I tend to rub or tap the following: crown, brow area, side of the eye, under the eye, under the nose / above the lip, middle of chin, below the collarbone, side of palm, index / thumb web (sometimes), and hugging the wrist of one hand with the other hand. Sometimes I rub or tap additional areas; sometimes I rub or tap very few areas.

Simply stated, rubbing or tapping releases the energetic hold your subconscious / unconscious mind uses to keep the thought / vibration in place within your mind and energy field. I believe the rubbing or tapping is a type of energetic pattern disruption.

Energy Clearing and Release Protocol for All Sessions

- Follow ***Beginning Session Protocol for All Divining Sessions.***
- Follow ***Divining Statements Protocol.***
- Follow ***Divining for More Information Protocol.***
- Follow ***Divining Which Clearing Modality to Use Protocol.***
- If ***Acu-Points Rub / Tap*** method is indicated, proceed.

Energetic Clearing and Release Procedures for a Negative / Challenged Statement[12]

This is the procedure to use if, when divining, you test *strong* (*yes*) regarding a Negative / Challenged Statement and are guided to use the *Acu-Points Rub / Tap* method.

- Using your fingertips, begin lightly rubbing or tapping (five or six circular rubs or taps ... or as many times as you are intuitively directed to rub or tap, or however long it takes for you to complete one of the statements below) on the meridian points suggested or indicated.
- While rubbing or tapping on each point, say (verbally or silently)—following your Intuition / Inner Guidance regarding which statement to say, when to say it, and so on—one or all of the following statements:
    - "Release. Release. Release."
    - "I release this energy from me now."
    - "Time to let this go."
    - "It is safe for me to let this go now."
    - Or say whatever else you feel, intuitively, you want to state.

NOTE: For me, most of the time it would take about three to six circular rubs or taps per point; other times it would take more than six. When uncertain, I would divine to discern how many circular rubs or taps would be best. It may vary from time to time. Follow your intuition.

Clearing and Releasing Inherited Energy Protocol (Acu-Points Rub / Tap Method)

If there was an indication for you to divine for more information and there was an indication that the energy / vibration was inherited, do more acu-point rubs / taps—more times than you usually

---

[12] If the statement energetic is inherited, refer to *Clearing and Releasing Inherited Energy Protocol for All Statements (Acu-Points Rub / Tap Method)* on pages 121-122.

would—and the amount that you are guided to do. Additionally, it may be beneficial to rub or tap more acu-points.

- At the same time, send a blessing to your ancestor.
- Visualize a cord being untied, a chain broken, a lock opening between you and your ancestor as it relates to that specific statement, or whatever else comes forward for you.
- You can also state things like:
    - "Release and go in peace."
    - "I honor and bless you. Be at peace. Now release."
    - Or whatever you feel your intuition is guiding you to state.

Confirm the Clearing and Release

- Refer to *How to Confirm the Release of a Negative / Challenged Statement Energetic Protocol.* (See pages 116–117.)

Energetic Clearing and Release Procedures for a Lack of Positive Statement[13]

This is the procedure to use if, when divining, you test *weak (no)* regarding a positive statement using the *Acu-Points Rub / Tap* method.

- While rubbing or tapping on each point, say (verbally or silently)—following your Intuition / Inner Guidance regarding which statement to say, when to say it, and so on—one or all of the following statements:
    - "It safe for me to experience ________________."
      Example: "It is safe for me to experience receiving money."
    - "I welcome the energy of ______________ now."
      Example: "I welcome the energy of receiving money now."

---

[13] If the statement energetic is inherited, refer to *Clearing and Releasing Inherited Energy Protocol for All Statements (Acu-Points Rub / Tap Method)* on pages 121–122 .

  - "It is for my maximum benefit to accept and experience ______________ now."
    Example: "It is for my maximum benefit to accept and experience *money liberation* now."
  - And/or whatever else you feel, intuitively, to state.
- Also, you can specifically address the blocks and/or imbalances:
  - "It is safe for me to remove all blocks and imbalances toward experiencing ______________ now."
  - And/or something similar. Follow your intuition.

Confirm the Clearing and Release

- Refer to *How to Confirm the Release of a Lack of Positive Statement Energetic Protocol.* (See pages 118–119.)

Other Energetic Clearing Modalities and Sources of Information

As mentioned earlier, you may be directed to use an additional or a different clearing and releasing modality or modalities. As always, use your Intuition / Inner Guidance and divine to discern which modality would be most beneficial at the time and each time you do this work. The modality you are directed to use may vary from session to session. It is important that you always check within.

Again, other sources of information include directly asking God / Spirit / Your Highest Power and by using your intuition. Affirm clarity. Always ask for guidance and support.

NOTE: When the time comes to do the clearing and release process, there may be times when you will be able to clear and release multiple statements; other times you'll only clear and release one or two. Be patient with yourself and with your process.

See *The Energetics of Money Liberation ~ The* PLAY*book—Support for Your Money Liberation Project* for specific examples and session suggestions.

Chapter 21

Step 6: Empower

Don't ask yourself what the world needs.
Ask yourself what makes you come alive, and go do that,
because what the world needs is people who have come alive.

—Howard Thurman

At this point in your *Money Liberation Project*, I want to offer suggestions to support you in positively reinforcing and shoring up any and all new and positive perspectives regarding money and the financial department in your life. Below are all things I have used and have found to be successful for reinforcing lessons learned, insights gleaned, and money relationship improvements (on my part).

Supportive Money Liberation—and Your New Relationship with Money Practices

Maintaining a positive relationship—with anyone and anything—requires time, energy, effort, positive focus, commitment, devotion, exploration, and honesty, just to name a few key elements. The same is true as it relates to improving your perceived relationship with money.

Here are some ways I have incorporated these elements:

- Meditating—listening to Inner Guidance
- Journaling—expressing my thoughts, feelings, and ideas
- Writing positive affirmations
- Setting my intentions, upon waking, regarding the quality of day I want to experience—and include aspects of *money liberations*

  - Examples: influx of financially qualified clients who see value and worth in my offerings—and who eagerly sign up for them, affiliate relationship opportunities / partnering, and so on
- Upon waking, expressing gratitude for what I already have—and for what is to come
- Prior to sleeping, expressing gratitude for what I have—and for what is to come
- Also prior to sleeping, setting my intention to enable my subconscious mind to relax during my sleep time and to enable blocks and/or imbalances to be cleared and released in an easy and gentle manner—and to wake refreshed and invigorated
- Socializing with energetically and spiritually uplifting people who are working toward self-betterment within their lives—including financially
- Getting additional support on all levels; some examples:
  - Spiritual: seeking spiritual counseling, prayer support
  - Seeking additional energetic healing
  - Consulting with a financial advisor

Regardless of your religion or denomination, here are some things you can do, energetically, to support yourself with your *money liberation*:

- Chant, recite mantras and affirmations.
- Sing or listen to uplifting songs and music.
- Listen to spiritually oriented, financially successful based inspirational and uplifting recordings.
- Attend spiritually based inspirational and uplifting workshops, seminars, and training programs.

While more suggestions and support materials can be found in *The Energetics of Money Liberation ~ The* PLAY*book—Support for Your Money Liberation Project*, what is listed above will be supportive ... and a great start.

Afterword

Both during and after completing my *Money Liberation Project*, I observed a myriad of different experiences, emotions, and results. While experiences will vary for each and every person who utilizes this program, I hope this section will shed some light on potential things you may or may not experience—although there are no promises or guarantees.

During both my "GOD Project" and *Money Liberation Project*, there were times during the clearing and releasing process that I burst out in tears. It was, as I experienced it, simply a release of old and stuck energy. I felt lighter (not so burdened or stressed) after the release. Sometimes I felt tired and had to take a nap.

What Really Matters

This is what matters: I experienced some negative / separation energy inside of me—between money and myself. I made a conscious and deliberate (intentional) decision to clear and release it via my *Money Liberation Project*. What *is* important is the direct, intimate, and profoundly loving experience of God / Spirit / My Highest Power—and the ever-present, loving and giving aspects of God's True Nature—and that includes financial resources.

The capital "T" Truth—as I experienced it:

- Negative energy was released.
- "Stories" are not important.
- This was not a mental "processing" experience.
- I do not need to mentally "figure this out."
- The clearing and releasing were real, visceral, and profound for me.
- I experienced clearing and releasing—on all levels.

I noticed positive shifts and a lightening / lifting of negative energy—especially compared to what I formerly experienced when I would think about money and what I want to achieve financially. Additionally, my financial resources grew significantly—and continue to do so.

After several times of doing clearing and releasing sessions, something profound happened. By clearing the energy associated with one particular Negative / Challenged Statement of a feeling / misperception I had about me as it relates to money, I felt a surge of energy come forward. It felt as if by clearing that one particular negative energy statement, a multitude of other negative / challenged energetic blocks and imbalances were simultaneously cleared and released. I had hit an inner "big kahuna"—the lynchpin that held a massive amount of separation energy within me toward me "receiving money—*now*!"

My mind wants to reason that multiple clearings and releasing happened at once, perhaps because the vibrations were attached at the same time, or perhaps they might have carried similar vibrations. It actually does not matter. Again, this not a mental process. No "story" or "figuring it out" is necessary or required. Actually, the creation of further stories only befuddles things by keeping me in my thinking mind. Knowing that to be true for myself and what I tend to do, I decided to simply own and embrace the clearing and releasing with gratitude. I suggest you do the same.

I have been asked numerous times why I could not or did not just find that one statement to begin with. This is what I have discovered: clearing and releasing is meant to be an easy and gentle process. By discerning (via asking within and divining) which energetic statement "needs" or "wants" to be cleared first, next, and so on, I believe it lays the groundwork for a more gentle, graceful, and grace-filled unfoldment and process.

Through doing this kind of work for a while, I also discovered that some energetic blocks and imbalances need to be cleared and released first and before all others—especially before the more deeply imbedded and entrenched blocks and imbalances can be cleared and released. I believe the initial clearings serve as "gatekeepers."

When the gatekeepers experience gentle clearing and releasing, it signals the psyche / ego that everything is fine—that it can relax a bit and it is safe to do this process. This then paves the way for other subconscious / unconscious "negative" energy blocks to ease up a bit, loosen their grip, and gently rise to the surface. It is almost as if each gatekeeper tests the waters to see if it can trust the process. The experience of a gentle process eases the psyche / ego, and it does not feel threatened. It senses it will not be damaged or annihilated; it will be safe; all is well—all will be well—and all can be even better.

All parts of this process have a purpose: the constant checking within by asking, via divining—"Is it safe and supportive to continue at this time?"... "Has this been released?"—and asking if more information is needed or wanted to be revealed; *plus* giving the hurt or wounded aspects inside respect, care, compassion, attention, and loving—are all part of the healing and transformational process. This is the means—the process—that assists in allowing the gatekeepers to relax—allowing the gates (which are keeping the "negative" / "lack of positive" energetics in place within) to open for clearing and releasing. I would even venture to say that a lack of the above (compassion, loving, respect, and so on) were most likely the reasons the energy became stuck in the first place. Embracing loving compassion and not making the energetic block and/or imbalance *wrong* or *bad* allowed the transformation I experienced.

One surprising discovery came as a result of doing both my "GOD Project" and *Money Liberation Project*. Prior to the commencement of each project, using the same method to discern what level of consciousness I scored (according to Dr. David R. Hawkins' "Map of Consciousness®" from his book *Power vs. Force*), I tested myself. I also tested myself after the completion of the major portion of my

"GOD Project" and again after my *Money Liberation Project.* The before-and-after results were astounding after my "GOD Project." Not only did my score increase, but it catapulted in a dramatic and astonishing way. Much to my surprise and delight, after my *Money Liberation Project*, my score increased as well.

My *Money Liberation Project*—like my "GOD Project"—will never end. As time passes, I still find some feelings and thoughts to clear and release, which I do on a regular basis. I release when they appear. Hopefully, you will do the same.

Another important aspect of my experience: Regardless of what I am emotionally experiencing and physically feeling on any given day, I now know that God's love is real, ever-present, and powerful. Additionally, as a daughter of the Most High, I know that my Heavenly Father wants to give me the Kingdom—and this is my birthright. As a beloved daughter of God, my birthright includes:

$ Money $

$ Continuous financial prosperity $

$ *Money liberation* $

Now!

I know that I know that I know—

I Am a beloved daughter of God, in whom God is well pleased.

I am loved and supported.

I am inherently worthy and have to "prove" nothing to anyone—
including God.

I know this is True for myself. I know this is True for you.

Money is energy—and supports me and my dreams,
goals, and desires.

I Am Grateful! I Am Grateful! I Am Grateful!

And so it is ...

Namaste.

—Dr. Linda Humphreys

Summary: Divining Steps and Energy Clearing and Releasing Protocols

Below you will find a list of steps and protocols that can assist you with the divining process and with the energetic clearing and releasing during your *Money Liberation Project*. (See pages 106–123 for detailed information.)

[14] If necessary, refer to the *Clearing and Releasing Inherited Energy Protocol for All Statements* on pp. 115–116.

[15] If necessary, refer to the *Clearing and Releasing Inherited Energy Protocol for All Statements* on pp. 115–116.

Some Fun Resources

Discover Your Sacred Money Archetypes®

I am excited about sharing some fun resources with you. The first is: Discover Your *Sacred Money Archetypes*®.

Archetypes, as I understand and use this term, are symbolic and iconic representations of personal characteristics and personality traits.

While you may be familiar with the concept of archetypes and are aware of your personal archetypes—did you know that we also have money archetypes? Well—we do!

The *Sacred Money Archetypes*® (SMA) assessment, created by Kendall Summerhawk, is an insightful tool used to assist with discovering your money archetypes. As an SMA Certified Coach, I am delighted to offer the SMA assessment to you—so that you can discover your top money archetype—for free!

Visit:

DrLindaHumphreys.com/Sacred-Money-Archetypes-SMA-Assessment

for more information—and to take your free assessment now!

Business Branding with Archetypes®

If you currently own and/or want to start your own business, another archetype-related resource offering is Business *Branding With Archetypes*®—another insightful assessment tool developed by Kendall Summerhawk.

In addition to having personal archetypes and money archetypes, did you know that your business has its own special and unique archetype super powers? Well—it does!

For more information about how I can assist you in identifying and clearly expressing your business's authentic brand and attracting your ideal clients / customers with your heart and soul-aligned branding and messaging, visit:

DrLindaHumphreys.com/Business-Branding-with-Archetypes

PLUS…

Money Liberation Coaching

Insightful!

Transformational!

Liberating!

Visit:

DrLindaHumphreys.com/Money-Liberation-Coaching

Bibliography

Biblegateway.com, website, *https://www.biblegateway.com*

Biblehub.com, website, *https://biblehub.com*

Brennan, Barbara Ann. *Hands of Light: A Guide to Healing Through the Human Energy Field: A New Paradigm for the Human Being in Health, Relationship, and Disease.* New York: Random House, 1988.

Byrne, Rhonda. *The Magic.* New York: Atria Books, 2012. Print.

Chapman University, "Voice of Wilkerson" page (blog), "America's Top Fears 2015," by Sheri Wilkerson, posted October 13, 2015. *https://blogs.chapman.edu/wilkinson/2016/10/11/americas-top-fears-2016/*

Dictionary.com, "abundance (n.)," accessed July 17, 2021 *https://www.dictionary.com/browse/abundance*

Dictionary.com, "abundantly (adv.)," accessed July 17, 2021 *https://www.dictionary.com/browse/abundantly*

Dictionary.com, "prosperous (n)," accessed July 17, 2021 *https://www.dictionary.com/browse/abundantly*

Emoto, Masaru. *The Hidden Messages in Water.* New York: Atria Books, 2011. Print.

Garman, Che. "Abundance Quotations." Affirm Your Life (blog). *http://affirmyourlife.blogspot.com/2011/06/abundance-quotations.html*

Goodreads "Abundance Quotes," website,
https://goodreads/quotes/tag/abundance.

Hawkins, David R. *Power vs. Force: The Hidden Determinants of Human Behavior, Author's Official Revised Edition.* San Diego: Hay House, 2012. Kindle edition, Chapter 3.

Hicks, Abraham. "When Launching Creative Rockets of Desire," March 25, 2011, YouTube video, 00:45,
https://www.youtube.com/watch?v=kfuszUBXNMc

Hicks, Esther and Jerry. *Ask and It Is Given: Learning to Manifest Your Desires.* San Diego: Hay House, 2006. Print.

Hicks, Esther and Jerry. *The Essential Law of Attraction Collection.* Hay House, 2013. E-book.

Hicks, Esther and Jerry. *The Vortex: Where the Law of Attraction Assembles All Cooperative Relationships.* San Diego: Hay House, 2009. Print.

Humphreys, Linda. *Getting God® ~ "The GOD Project"—6 Steps for Divining Your Way to a More Intimate & Loving Relationship with God.* Inside Out Transformation, 2019.

Humphreys, Linda. *Getting God® ~ The Guidebook—Exploration & Conscious Connection Support for Your "GOD Project."* Inside Out Transformation, 2019.

Humphreys, Linda. *The Energetics of Money Liberation™ ~ The* PLAY*book—Support for Your Money Liberation Project.* Inside Out Transformation, 2022.

Lindner, Melanie. "What People Are Still Willing to Pay For." Forbes, website, January 15, 2009.
https://www.forbes.com/2009/01/15/self-help-industry-ent-sales-cx_ml_0115selfhelp.html?sh=3d8776696758

Myers, Lindsay. "The Self-Help Industry Helps Itself to Billions of Dollars." Brainblogger website, May 23, 2014. *https://brainblogger.com/2014/05/23/the-self-help-industry-helps-itself-to-billions-of-dollars/*

NPD Group. "Self Help Book Sales Are Rising Fast in the US, The NPD Group Says," website, January 13, 2020. *https://www.npd.com/news/press-releases/2020/self-help-book-sales-are-rising-fast-in-the-us-the-npd-group-says/*

Osteen, Joel. *Become a Better You: 7 Keys to Improving Your Life Every Day.* New York: Howard Books, 2009.

Osteen, Joel. *Your Best Life Now: 7 Steps to Living at Your Full Potential.* FaithWorks, 2015.

Summerhawk, Kendall. Branding With Archetypes®. Heart of Success, 2021.

Summerhawk, Kendall. Sacred Money Archetypes®. Heart of Success, 2021.

United Nations University, "Richest 2% Own half the World's Wealth; Study," news release no. 44: December 2006–February 2007. *https://archive.unu.edu/update/issue44_22.htm*

Williamson, Marianne. *A Return to Love: Reflections on the Principles of A Course of Miracles.* New York: HarperCollins, 1992.

Acknowledgments

Thank you
God / Spirit / My Higher Power—without whom I could not do anything.
I am in awe, deeply humbled and grateful for
the miraculous positive transformations in my life.

To my teachers and "way-show-ers":
Dr. Seuss (aka: Theodor Seuss Geisel)
Abraham Lincoln
The Pathwork
Dr. Carl Rogers
Dr. Carl Jung
Marianne Williamson
A Course in Miracles
Rev. Dr. Martin Luther King, Jr.
Rev. Dr. Michael Beckwith
Dr. Paul Barrett
Conversations with God
Drs. Ron and Mary Hulnick
Dr. Caroline Myss
Dr. Joe Dispenza
Dr. Robert Holden

To my dear friends, who made me laugh—especially at myself.

To my "spiritual friends"—
my "nudge-rs" / "prodders" / "stackers" / "thorns in my side"
through whom I have learned some of my greatest spiritual lessons along the way.
Y'all know who you are. ☺

To Jeff—
a source of an abundance of great love,
joy, fun, adventure, laughter, and support.

And, as always …
Thank you, BABY JESUS!!!

Amen.

About the Author

I am a seeker.

I am a perpetual student.

I make mistakes.

As a seeker and student, I have learned from my mistakes and am now making conscious strides to "choose again," as *A Course in Miracles* suggests.

I believe in releasing any / all perceived internal confines (judgments, misperceptions)—especially related to the past.

I believe in all forms of forgiveness—including self-forgiveness.

I believe in learning lessons, releasing the past—and moving on.

I believe in being grounded in the present moment because this is where the magic happens. I strive to be present—to fully show up and be "all in"—in all I do.

I believe in being more loving and compassionate toward myself and others in the present—which sets the tone for a more love-filled present—and paves the way for a more love-filled future.

I made a commitment to transform—on all levels.

I strive for personal excellence.

I believe in change, transformation, miracles, and the power of Love.

I view my transformed life as a miracle.

I made a commitment to support others in their transformation and support them in experiencing their own miracles.

My zodiac sign is Gemini.

My "birth card" is Ace of Clubs.

My Enneagram test revealed that I have many personality tendencies (with "tied" scores in both my number one and two positions)—with lots of "wings" to support me.

I don't expect other people to "figure me out" because I can't "figure" myself out.

I tell those I love to "strap on your seat belt" and enjoy the ride when they are with me.

I love flowers.
Tulips make me smile.
I love the scent of carnations.
Laughter makes me laugh.
I love to laugh.
I love spending time with friends.
I believe in "retail therapy."
I love new adventures.
I love delightful surprises.
I love traveling and meeting new people.
I love 70 percent dark chocolate, Utz Potato Chips, and eating Maryland crab … anything.
I love to eat.

I love my various families, tribes, and peeps.
I love my husband.
I love America.
I love the entire universe.
I love children.
I love God.
I love "Baby Jesus."
I love you.

Linda Humphreys, PhD
DrLindaHumphreys.com

Index

Made in United States
Orlando, FL
11 November 2026

90609398R00095